PICTURE BRIDE, WAR BRIDE

Picture Bride, War Bride

The Role of Marriage in Shaping Japanese America

Sonia C. Gomez

NEW YORK UNIVERSITY PRESS
New York

NEW YORK UNIVERSITY PRESS
New York
www.nyupress.org

Parts of chapter 1 was previously published in *Amerasia Journal*. It has been reproduced here with permission. Parts of chapter 3 was published in the *Journal of American Ethnic History*. It has been reproduced here with permission.

Library of Congress Cataloging-in-Publication Data
Names: Gomez, Sonia C. (Sonia Christine), author.
Title: Picture bride, war bride : the role of marriage in shaping Japanese America / Sonia C. Gomez.
Other titles: Role of marriage in shaping Japanese America
Description: New York : New York University Press, [2024] | Includes bibliographical references and index. | Summary: "Picture Bride, War Bride: The Role of Marriage in Shaping Japanese America examines how the institution of marriage created pockets of legal and social inclusion for Japanese women in the United States during periods of racial exclusion"—Provided by publisher.
Identifiers: LCCN 2023040744 (print) | LCCN 2023040745 (ebook) |
ISBN 9781479803071 (hardback) | ISBN 9781479803088 (ebook other) |
ISBN 9781479803095 (ebook)
Subjects: LCSH: Japanese American women—Cultural assimilation. | Japanese—United States—History—20th century. | Intercountry marriage—United States. | Japanese Americans—Social life and customs. | Women immigrants—United States—History—20th century. | Immigrants—United States—History—20th century. | War brides—United States—History. | Mail order brides—United States—History.
Classification: LCC E184.J3 G66 2024 (print) | LCC E184.J3 (ebook) |
DDC 973/.04956—dc23/eng/20240307
LC record available at https://lccn.loc.gov/2023040744
LC ebook record available at https://lccn.loc.gov/2023040745

New York University Press books are printed on acid-free paper, and their binding materials are chosen for strength and durability. We strive to use environmentally responsible suppliers and materials to the greatest extent possible in publishing our books.

Manufactured in the United States of America

10 9 8 7 6 5 4 3 2 1

Also available as an ebook

For my family

CONTENTS

Introduction

In the summer of 1869, the first Japanese migrants arrived on the mainland United States and made their way to Coloma, California—a small town in Gold Country just outside Sacramento. There were twenty-two in all, over half of them allegedly former samurai. Accompanied by Henry Schnell, a Prussian diplomat and trader who had spent time in Japan, and his Japanese wife, Jou, they left their ancestral homeland in search of economic opportunities. They expected to find fertile farmland that would eventually lead to wealth. These settler migrants planted mulberry trees, rice, bamboo, and tea they brought with them from Japan, establishing the Wakamatsu Tea and Silk Colony.[1] But they soon learned that the land was difficult to cultivate.[2] After two years, the 272-acre settlement was abandoned. One by one they moved on, most returning to Japan. Only three of the original settlers remained: Matsunoke Sakurai continued to eke out an existence on the arid land and later went to work for the Veerkamp family, who eventually took over the settlement after it was abandoned; Kuninosuke Masumizu went on to marry a mixed-race Black and native woman named Carrie Wilson; and Okei Ito, a nineteen-year-old woman who worked as a nursemaid for the Schnell family and later for the Veerkamp family. Ito fell ill in 1871 and died soon after. She was buried at the top of a small hill on the Wakamatsu farm where a tombstone erected in her honor stands. Ito was the first known Japanese native to have died on American soil.[3]

Today the Wakamatsu Tea and Silk Colony is a registered California historic landmark and viewed by some as the Plymouth Rock of Japanese America.[4] Although she never had biological children, Okei Ito has been described as the mother of Japanese immigration. Jou Schnell, on the other hand, the Japanese wife of Henry Schnell, arrived in the US with one child and delivered another in 1870 at Wakamatsu. Though Jou and Henry Schnell's mixed-race daughter was likely the first child of a Japanese parent born on American soil, Jou is not considered the mother of Japanese immigration, and no records have been found indicating what happened to Henry and Jou Schnell or their children after they left Wakamatsu. [5] The lives of these two women, Okei Ito and Jou Schnell, and the varied extent to which they have each been memorialized, reveals the ways in which gender, motherhood, and marriage shaped Japanese migration to the United States from the start.[6] Further, that one of the first Japanese migrants to settle in the United States, Kuninosuke Masumizu, married a mixed-race woman and fathered three children points to the heterogeneous racial origins of the Japanese in America. Interracial intimacies have shaped the Japanese experience in America from the beginning.

After the end of the Wakamatsu colony, Japanese migration to the continental United States occurred in distinct patterns distinguished by gender. Those first to voyage across the Pacific in large numbers were men, primarily laborers. Japanese women followed soon after. Beginning in the 1870s and increasing throughout the late nineteenth and early twentieth centuries, young Japanese men migrated to the United States in unprecedented numbers. Many were from farming families that had been displaced after the Meiji Restoration in 1868. They came to advance their economic standing with the hopes of returning home after a few years of work and accumulated wealth. Many, however, settled in the West and eventually started families. Most of those who settled did so by summoning wives from Japan in arranged proxy marriages. In many cases, the bride and groom had only corresponded through letters and photographs. Relatives in Japan matched men and women who they believed would be a good fit for companionship, then the couples would wed in Japan with the grooms in absentia. This practice complemented traditional Japanese marriage customs that relied on trusted local matchmakers to arrange marriages. Once the bride arrived in the US, her husband would meet her at the arriving dock where US officials would officiate the marriage.[7] This time, however, the unions were recognized by US law. These transpacific marriages and the arrival of Japanese women, known as picture brides, were made possible by the Gentlemen's Agreement of 1908.

The Gentlemen's Agreement of 1908 was designed to halt the migration of Japanese laboring men, but an exception was made for the wives of Japanese men already in the United States. Thus, after 1908, Japanese women began to immigrate in large numbers. Like the men they married, many of the women were from farming families. Some came from middle-class families. Many were literate and educated. The women were usually in their late teens to early twenties. Some migrated out of desperation, others sought adventure and opportunity. Simply put, Japanese women migrants came from a variety of backgrounds, and though their lives in the US shared many similarities, their lived experiences varied.[8]

The Gentlemen's Agreement produced a paradox of inclusion and exclusion for the Japanese. The agreement excluded Japanese male laborers from entering the US, while at the same time it allowed Japanese brides to enter. Yet this nuance is lost in much of the scholarship on the Gentlemen's Agreement, which has focused primarily on the exclusion of men. An anti-Japanese movement on the West Coast emerged as soon as Japanese migrants stepped foot on American soil. Many exclusionists had been involved in the anti-Chinese movement in the previous years. Lobbying Congress to pass a national policy of Japanese exclusion, as they did with the Chinese, the exclusionists fought long and hard to null the Gentlemen's Agreement and abolish the picture bride migration it encouraged. The National Origins Act of 1924 did just that. Picture bride migration came to a slow halt in 1921, then a complete stop by 1924.

Then, immediately following World War II, Japanese women began to migrate to the US again, this time as the "war brides" of American servicemen abroad.[9] Though they were restricted from entering per the National Origins Act of 1924, a series of postwar war bride acts created a narrow path of entrance. Once again Japanese women were permitted to enter the US as brides. This book interrogates the role marriage played in the formation of Japanese America. For some, marriage was a means of inclusion, albeit a highly contested and conditional inclusion. For others, marriage was a means of exclusion. Marrying the wrong person or not marrying at all restricted one's status in Japanese America.

A Gendered Diaspora

Picture Bride, War Bride explores the distinct gendered nature of Japanese migration which constitutes what I call a *gendered diaspora.*[10] The term "diaspora" derives from the Greek word, *diaspeirein*, meaning to disperse, scatter, or spread about. Historically, the term has been used to describe the forced exile of Jewish people. In the middle of the twentieth century, the term's usage expanded to describe the enslavement and dispersal of Africans during the transatlantic slave trade. Today, "diaspora" has been adopted by scholars of transnational migration more broadly to refer to migrants and their descendants who identify with a "homeland" but live outside of it. This identification manifests in cultural practices, food, language, community, and affective ties. While diaspora produces a sense of belonging to a "homeland" it also produces a sense of un-belonging in the adopted country or place of residence. The term "diaspora" is used here as both descriptive marker and analytical category. The term's analytical reach rests largely on its ability to deal with specific problems related to the transnational migration of people.[11]

The term *gendered* is used to refer to the ways in which immigration policies and practices shape and are shaped by ideas, attitudes, and practices regarding gender and sexual norms at the national and local level. Thus, a *gendered diaspora* is based on the conviction that gender shapes migration and diaspora, and conversely migration and diaspora shapes gender. Because the first wave of Japanese to arrive on US soil were primarily young, able-bodied men seeking work, wealth, and adventure, the scholarship on Japanese migration before World War II is dominated by a discussion of these men and the race-based exclusion that came soon after their arrival. The tendency to ignore questions of gender in the study of Japanese migration obscures the ways in which ideas about the proper role of men, women, and the nuclear family shaped inclusion and exclusion for Japanese migrants in America.[12] *Picture Bride, War Bride* shows how racial *and* gendered logic converged to shape immigration patterns for the Japanese in the United States.[13] It challenges the dominant periodization of Japanese American history by analyzing the prewar migration of picture brides alongside the postwar migration of war brides.

Building on the work of sociologist Catherine Lee, this book interrogates how "race *making* and gender construction were constitutive of immigration control" in the case of Japanese immigration to the United States.[14] In her comparative analysis of Chinese and Japanese exclusion, Lee argues that a failure to see immigrant exclusion as a "gendered process of racialization [produces] a view of immigration policy as an instrument of racialization alone." Viewing immigration policy through a racial lens only distorts the historical meanings and practices of Japanese immigration to the United States, for, as Lee argues, "how and why men and women immigrate, for what purposes, in what familial and/or sexual relations, and under which regulatory control by the state have important consequences for how a perceived ethnoracial collective may settle and affirm or challenge the existing notion of the family writ large—the nation."[15] This is true of nearly all immigrant groups in the United States.

Marriage, as both a social and political institution, served as a mechanism of inclusion and exclusion for the Japanese in the United States. In the case of migration before World War II, marriage determined who would be allowed to enter and who would be included in Japanese American communities. By virtue of the Gentlemen's Agreement of 1908, Japanese women were permitted entry as wives, facilitating settlement and the emergence of the Nisei—the American-born children of Japanese immigrants. Japanese women were so critical to Japanese success in the US that the elite Japanese Americans who promoted settlement worked closely with officials in Japan to prepare the women for what lay ahead.[16] In contrast, those Japanese men who did not marry and send for wives lived their lives on the margins. After World War II, marriage, again, served as the primary mode of incorporation for Japanese women, but this time it also served as a pathway to citizenship, in addition to new modes of local and national belonging for the thousands of Japanese women who married American servicemen and made homes in the United States.

Marriage has the power to shape belonging on a local and national scale for immigrants in America. As historian Nancy Cott explains, on a national scale, state-sanctioned marriage weds the couple to one another and weds them to the state. Married couples gain certain rights and privileges, such as a pathway to citizenship, tax credits, and inheritance of property. But the couple must also fulfill their obligations to the state, mostly by preserving the sanctimony of marriage in the form of husbands' financial support of wives, ensuring neither become charges of the state.[17] The reciprocal relationship between married couples and the state legitimizes these unions and incorporates them as family units into the nation-state.[18] As a social institution, marriage has the power to legitimize some unions while rendering others illegitimate and thus unnatural. Peggy Pascoe asserts that by recognizing some unions and enfolding them into the nation-state, the state defines the parameters of respectable and unrespectable romance and kinship.[19] Marriage is an institution that can also exclude. It has both constructive and destructive power. This power is clearly evident in immigration law and practice. For marriage migrants, marital regulations legitimize relationships by recognizing them in the eyes of the law, thereby defining who is and is not a member of the family unit, community, and state. By contrast, those not protected by the state through marriage remain excluded and vulnerable to deportation.

In 1950, Thomas Radtke, a native of Chicago and member of the US Armed Forces who served in both Japan and Korea, petitioned Congress to pass special legislation to permit Mitsuko Ito a temporary visa to enter the country. Ito was Radtke's Japanese fiancé and was excluded from entering the US per the National Origins Act of 1924, which excluded Asian migration on the basis of race. Because Radtke and Ito were not yet married under American law, she was not permitted to enter under the auspices of the War Bride Act of 1947, which allowed Japanese women to bypass the Origins Act if they were brides of American servicemen. Radtke called upon his state congressman for assistance. Private Law 614, which allowed Ito entry into the US, was approved on June 28, 1950. However, the terms were conditional. Mitsuko Ito was given three months to marry Radtke and apply for permanent residence in order to prove her "bona fide intention" to marry an American; otherwise, she would face deportation.[20] In other words, as a Japanese woman, Mitsuko was an alien inadmissible because of race. However, as the wife of an American serviceman, she was permitted entry and permanent residency. Therefore, marriage legitimized Mitsuko's presence in the United States thereby articulating the boundaries of belonging between herself, Radtke, and the state.

More precisely, Japanese women's migration to the US was a process of *differential inclusion*. In Yen Le Espiritu's work on the Filipino/a diaspora she maintains that Filipinos/as in the US were not wholly excluded because as a group, they were deemed integral to the nation's economy, culture, identity, and power. But their inclusion was predicated on their subordinated status.[21] Similarly, at times, Japanese women have been conditionally included. Their entry was made possible—and in the post-World War II era desirable—because of their labor, both intimate and reproductive. In the United States, Japanese women were valued for what their racialized bodies could offer the nation.

Chapter Outline

Traditionally, the story of Japanese immigration to the United States has been a story about the West Coast. *Picture Bride, War Bride*, however, is a national history of the Japanese in America. As such, it is organized thematically, and as a result moves around in place and time. It begins on the West Coast with the arrival of picture brides in 1908 and then moves to Chicago in the post-World War II era to examine the lives of Issei men who remained unwed and on the periphery. It moves next to Japan in the postwar era to examine the circumstances that created the second wave of Japanese women's migration. Finally, it examines the experiences and legacy of Japanese war brides in postwar America, a history particularly robust in the Midwest.

Chapter one, "A Paradox of Exclusion: Women, Family, and Reproduction in Early Japanese America," examines the first wave of Japanese women's migration to the United States in the early twentieth century after the Gentlemen's Agreement of 1908. It recasts the agreement as not only a mechanism of exclusion, which is how it is traditionally described by historians, but one that had the power to both include and exclude. After detailing the gendered process of migration for Japanese women, this chapter examines the role of gender in the anti-Japanese movement that catalyzed soon after the women's arrival. The popular and political discourse of the era are analyzed to reveal how Japanese exclusion was in large part a reaction to Japanese women's labor power, both reproductive and productive. For example, the perceived threat of Japanese women's reproductive labor (i.e., their birth rate) is notably observed in the inflammatory rhetoric of anti-Japanese politicians like California senator James Phelan. The discussion of productive labor shows how Japanese women's work in and out of the home was presented as an economic threat to white American families (the fact that much of Japanese women's labor was unpaid was of no concern to exclusionists).

Chapter two, "Issei Bachelors: Unmarried Men at the Margins," analyzes the lives of Japanese immigrant men—so called Issei bachelors—who never married nor had children and as a result lived their lives on the margins of society. In focusing on these men, the chapter demonstrates how marriage functioned as a mode of exclusion for those who did not marry. The chapter follows the lives of four Issei bachelors who resettled in Chicago after World War II, and explores the various reasons—sexuality, social and economic status, migratory work patterns—why Issei bachelors did not marry. Issei bachelors never fully incorporated into larger Japanese American communities—let alone mainstream American society—and remained intimately tied to their ancestral homeland.

Chapter three, "The US Occupation of Japan and the Making of Postwar Japanese America," turns to the post-World War II migration of Japanese women. It examines the racial politics of the Allied Occupation of Japan and the interracial encounters that emerged. It also reveals the ways that marriage legitimatized Japanese women's immigration to the US in the postwar period (as it had in the early twentieth century) by focusing on the active role American servicemen in Japan took in influencing immigration reform.

Chapter four, "'A Bridge Between East and West': Domesticity and Citizenship in the Making of Japanese War Brides" focuses on the ways that marriage and domesticity as a state apparatus legitimized national and local belonging of Japanese women in the postwar era. It begins by examining American Red Cross bride schools in Japan and the United States, demonstrating how the bride schools, along with US State Department propaganda and America's Cold War obsession with the East, created a milieu in which Japanese war brides became the symbol of ideal postwar domesticity reflecting the prewar Japanese concept of the "Good Wife, Wise Mother" (*ryōsai kenbo*).

Finally, chapter five, "Goodwill Ambassadors: Japanese War Brides in Postwar America" examines the ways Japanese war brides in the United States organized themselves in an attempt to negotiate their multilayered identities: Japanese woman, American wife and mother; recent enemy, Cold War ally. It focuses on the Cosmo Club, a Japanese war bride club founded in 1952 Chicago, as well as similar clubs throughout the United States, wherein the women positioned themselves as ambassadors between the US and Japan as a way to combat racial discrimination, negotiate their racial identity in a climate dominated by the Black and white binary, and fortify US-Japan relations. Finally, it explores the precarious position of Japanese war brides married to African American servicemen who often took on the racial status of their husbands and were excluded because of their intimate ties to Black communities.

Counter-Narratives and Alternative Histories

Japanese immigration to the United States began with the 1882 Chinese Exclusion Act, which prohibited Chinese laborers from entering the United States. The act was the culmination of a decades-long campaign crafted by white, working-class men and their political allies to rid the American West of the "Yellow Peril." It was the first legislation that barred immigration to the US solely on the basis of race and class. Subsequently, Japanese laborers were recruited to work in the fields, mines, hotels, and homes of the American West to take the place of the Chinese.

Upon arriving in the US, poor Japanese immigrant men worked a variety of low-paying, back-breaking jobs. They labored on the railroads of Utah and Montana, in the agriculture fields of California's Central Valley, as cooks in Alaskan mines, and as hotel boys, bartenders, and domestic hands in San Francisco, Los Angeles, and Seattle. Some realized their dream and returned to Japan in triumph while others permanently settled in the United States. Kenichi Sakoda, for example, came to America with his older brother around 1902 when he was just a teenager. The Sakoda brothers were from a large, poor farm family from the village of Funakoshi located in Hiroshima. After arriving in Seattle, the two young men worked as laborers and eventually moved on to the railroads of Montana. They ultimately settled in California, attracted by lucrative farming opportunities and warm weather. In California they were joined by a younger brother. Kenichi Sakoda briefly returned to Japan to marry a Japanese woman. Together they had three children. Along with his wife and brothers, Kenichi Sakoda worked as a poultry farmer, alfalfa harvester, dairy operator, hog farmer, and junk collector. Kenichi's two brothers returned to Japan with the money they had saved working in the United States after a barn fire destroyed the Sakoda family's dairy enterprise. In Japan they found success starting a scrap steel business. The youngest Sakoda brother would go on to become the mayor of Funakoshi.[22]

The return migration of Kenichi Sakoda's brothers underscores the temporary nature of Japanese immigration to America in the early twentieth century when close to 33 percent of all Japanese returned home. According to economist Masao Suzuki, the return rate of Japanese immigrants between 1920 and 1930 was more than 85 percent.[23] Although a large number of Japanese did settle in the US, it was their intention—at least in the early days of their arrival—to return to Japan.[24] In this way, the Sakoda brothers' return to Japan was emblematic of what one hoped to achieve by going abroad to work. Kenichi Sakoda's life in America, on the other hand, is the story of Japanese America.

After his brothers returned to Japan, Kenichi Sakoda moved his family to Gardena, a working-class suburb of Los Angeles, but the family eventually found their way to the outskirts of Little Tokyo. After many hardships, including pervasive discrimination and wartime incarceration, the Sakoda family went on to live productive, meaningful lives. James Sakoda, Kenichi's second son, sat down with oral historian Arthur Hansen to tell his family's history in 1988, seven years after he retired from a professorship in the sociology department at Brown University.

The story of the Sakoda family is ultimately one of triumph. It is one of many that highlight both the injustices experienced by the Japanese in America and their hard-earned successes afterwards. Although the Sakoda family suffered at the hands of whites and were grossly mistreated by the state and common folk alike, their story—and the pervasive retelling of similar stories—obscures the lives of others who were not so fortunate as to achieve postwar success.

Picture Bride, War Bride is not about the lives of those like the Sakodas. Instead, it is a history of those at the margins. The pages that follow trace the lives of Japanese immigrant women, including those who married across the color line in the post-World War II period, as well as the lives of unmarried Japanese American men. It is a retelling of history that examines the ways in which gender and sexuality shaped Japanese immigration and settlement in the United States challenging the well-known narrative of the Japanese in America.

1

A Paradox of Exclusion

Women, Family, and Reproduction in Early Japanese America

We gave birth during the Year of the Monkey
We gave birth during the Year of the Rooster.
We gave birth during the Year of the Dog
and the Dragon and the Rat.
—Julie Otsuka, *The Buddha in the Attic*

On December 10, 1910, twenty-year-old Yoshi Kiyomura arrived at Angel Island in the San Francisco Bay aboard the *Chiyo Maru*. Upon her arrival, Kiyomura was questioned by immigration officials about her background in Japan and plans for life in America. Authorities were particularly interested in her marriage to Masaki Kiyomura, a native of Japan who had immigrated to the US in 1901 and lived and worked in Gardena, a rural community in Southern California. Immigration officials also questioned Masaki, who had been awaiting Kiyomura's arrival to Angel Island. Masaki assured the interrogators that he had made all the necessary preparations to receive Kiyomura: "I have a house ready for her," he explained. Among the questions asked of all arriving Japanese women and their awaiting spouses was the question of labor. "What do you intend to do here if admitted?" the immigration inspector asked Mrs. Kiyomura. "Household work," she answered. "What do you intend to have your wife do if admitted?" the inspector asked Mr. Kiyomura. "Household duties only," he answered.[1] Traditional gender roles and a belief in a sharp division of labor were central to gender relations in the US in the early twentieth century. For Japanese immigrant women, such expectations were heightened, evidenced by the interrogation of Mr. and Mrs. Kiyomura and others like them.[2]

Women like Mrs. Kiyomura were permitted to enter the US as wives to Japanese men already in the United States. In the eyes of immigration officials, they were expected to be distinct from laborers who were barred from entering the US in the Gentleman's Agreement of 1908. As such they and their husbands had to be careful not to reveal any information that would deviate from the rules that governed their entrance. Likewise, their husbands had to be sure to not reveal as much. All parties involved assumed household chores did not constitute labor. Yoshi Kiyomura's experience at Angel Island is not unusual. Thousands of Japanese women went through the same process of interrogation, a process predominantly concerned with their roles as wives, mothers, and potential wage earners, revealing the ways in which the productive and reproductive labor of women was a source of deep concern for immigration officials.

Political discourse on the "problem" of Japanese immigration during the first two decades of the twentieth century demonstrates how ideas about race, gender, sexuality, and labor converged to create a paradox of inclusion and exclusion for the Japanese in America. The Gentlemen's Agreement, a series of negotiations between the US and Japan beginning in 1907 and ending in 1908, defined the terms of Japanese immigration from 1908 to 1921. The agreement prohibited Japanese laboring men from entering the country. Traditionally, historians have described the agreement as marking the beginning of a series of policies to exclude the Japanese from the national polity. By making the primary focus the exclusion of men, many scholars have failed to attend to the gendered dimensions of the agreement.[3] To be sure, the agreement was an exclusionist measure created in response to the white nativists in California who had been agitating loudly and violently for the total exclusion of the Japanese.[4] However, significant exceptions were made. Merchants, students, and tourists continued to be permitted entry, as well as laborers who were former residents of the US, and the business partners of settled Japanese farmers. More importantly, the parents, wives, and children of Japanese laborers living in the United States were also allowed to enter. This final exception facilitated the migration of more than 36,000 Japanese women, making family, community, and permanent settlement possible for many.[5] The Gentlemen's Agreement carried inclusionary and exclusionary power.

The Gentlemen's Agreement and later the National Origins Act, which barred the arrival of all Japanese immigrants including wives, were fraught with gendered politics and eugenicist thinking. While the

1908 agreement allowed Japanese migrant men to bring wives to the US and create normative nuclear families—if they had the means and will to do so—the 1924 National Origins Act marked the end of that possibility. Indeed, for many single Japanese men, state-sanctioned heterosexual intimacy and companionship would lie out of reach for years to come while for others it would never materialize. The 1924 act represents a crucial turning point in US immigration history, specifically for the Japanese, as it marks the complete victory of anti-Japanese politicians in the West to shape a national policy of total exclusion regardless of gender or family status.

Before the mass arrival of Japanese women, nativists focused their energy on Japanese men who they believed threatened the economic security and sexual purity of white families, the racial purity of white women, and the sexual authority of white men.[5] After 1908, nativists turned their attention to women like Yoshi Kiyomura. Attacks on Japanese women were not simply an extension of the anti-Japanese rhetoric used in the previous decades, but rather point to a fundamental development in the ways in which women's bodies were used throughout the twentieth century to either incite hostility in the populace or, as seen in the post-World War II era, bolster the state. Historically women reproduce the nation-state, as "intergenerational transmitters of cultural traditions, customs, songs, cuisine, and, of course, the mother tongue," they play a significant role in shaping the nation as migration scholar Nira Yuval-Davis has explained.[6] In the case of immigrant women, past and present, the burden of reproduction poses a particular threat to nativists, for the children they bear on American soil are entitled to birthright citizenship, as enshrined in the Fourteenth Amendment of the United States Constitution.

Anti-Japanese language in the period of the Gentlemen's Agreement reflected a fear, at times a paranoia, of Japanese women's reproduction. In California and other parts of the West, anti-Japanese politicians orchestrated a gender panic that specifically targeted Japanese women at a time when birth rates amongst white American women were declining and immigration from Japan and southern and eastern European was climbing.[7] The attack on Japanese women was an attempt to achieve political hegemony in the West at a time when white American dominance was threatened. The anti-Japanese movement was highly localized and focused on rural agricultural areas of California where the number of Japanese immigrants was the largest. By 1924, what began as a regional conflict had grown into a national policy of exclusion.

Rethinking the Gentlemen's Agreement

Immigration historians tend to describe the Gentlemen's Agreement as a compromise between President Roosevelt's desire to appease California nativists who had grown loud in their disapproval of his ambiguous stance on Japanese immigration, and his desire to maintain diplomatic relations with Japan. When Japan defeated the Russian empire in the Russo-Japanese war in 1905, it became the first non-white nation in modern history to defeat a white nation. Japan's growing military and industrial power bolstered its status on the global stage. Japanese officials were keen to flex their nation's newly developed muscle to secure protections for Japanese nationals living and laboring in the United States. However, as the story goes, at best, Roosevelt had not fully understood that by allowing the wives of Japanese men entry, the US had inadvertently created a "loophole" that encouraged the mass migration of Japanese women.[8] The loophole argument was made popular by Japanese exclusionists and has been taken for granted by historians who have reproduced it in scholarship. Anti-Japanese lobbyists claimed Japanese men in America were exploiting the family provision loophole in the Gentlemen's Agreement because many Japanese picture brides engaged in work outside the home. They argued that the arrival of women undermined the agreement's efforts to abolish economic competition for white men. In sending for their wives, Japanese men in America were accused of sending for laborers.

However, the exceptions made in the Gentlemen's Agreement did not occur in a vacuum nor do they not constitute a loophole. Defined by the Oxford English Dictionary as "an ambiguity or inadequacy in the law or a set of rules," the term loophole obscures the ways in which government officials on both sides of the Pacific valued the role of the family in immigration policies and practices. Why were parents, wives, and children desirable, while others were not? Why did an exclusionary measure, one that would lead to further restrictions, include an exception that allowed, indeed encouraged, Japanese family formation in the US?

Roosevelt and the American diplomats involved in the negotiations understood that those who were to be excluded—Japanese laboring men—posed an economic threat to white laborers and farmers on the West Coast and a sexual threat to white men and women. Their racial and cultural differences were believed to be evidence that they were "unassimilable" and thus "undesirable." By contrast, those who were permitted to immigrate—parents, wives, and children—were believed to possess the potential to assimilate and were thus deemed desirable. Catherine Lee has argued that "family ideation"—defined as the idealized conceptualization of the family based on traditional gender roles, sexual norms, class ideals, and racial and ethnic characteristics—was embedded in informal and formal immigration policies during the period of the Gentlemen's Agreement, as evidenced by the immigration process for women like Kiyomura.[9] Family ideation created a "liminal space" in which Japanese immigrant men with financial and social means could make use of the family provisions outlined in the agreement thereby sponsoring the arrival of family members who were otherwise excluded.[10]

While the Agreement was indeed an attempt to quell the rising criticism coming from the West Coast, it was also a diplomatic gesture to acknowledge Japan as a member of the "family of nations," as Republican senator George Pepper explained in 1924.[11] By allowing Japanese immigrant men the opportunity to sponsor the arrival of family members, the US recognized Japan as a peer nation whose citizens were worthy of marriage and family, and all the privileges the two institutions confer.[12] However, it was an empty gesture for Japanese nationals, who were barred from naturalizing until the 1952 McCarran–Walter Act.[13] Further, the Gentlemen's Agreement, in name and in practice, relied upon Victorian ideas about gender roles, sexuality, and the nuclear family that subjugated women to men. In California and elsewhere in the West, nativists promoted a gendered logic wherein white women were tasked with inspiring men to behave well and seek upward mobility.[14] Using the same logic, the Gentlemen's Agreement assumed Japanese women would turn single Japanese men into devoted husbands and fathers. The latter were less a threat. Such ideas were so accepted by the men who negotiated the Gentlemen's Agreement that the exception for parents, wives, and children did not warrant any elaboration, justification, or comment.[15] According to scholar Eithne Luibhéld, the agreement carried "heteropatriarchal assumptions" that reinforced Japanese women's domesticity and dependency. Indeed, the presence of women would largely transform bachelor societies into model immigrant communities made up of heterosexual nuclear families. The Gentlemen's Agreement was only the first measure to control the channels through which Japanese women were admitted to the United States. In the post-World War II era, the Alien Brides Act, which also made a provision for the entry of Japanese women as brides only, sought to reinforce Japanese women's sexual respectability and willingness to conform to distinct gender roles.[16]

Labor and Intimacy: The Threat of Japanese Masculinity

In 1908, Roosevelt and friends most certainly understood what was at stake. In the first decades of the twentieth century when immigration policymakers argued over the problem of Japanese immigration, marriage and intimacy were key issues.[17] At the center of much of the debate after 1908 was whether Japanese picture bride immigration was resolving or exacerbating the Japanese "problem." In 1921, John P. Irish, a farmer, journalist, and politician, testified before the Congressional Committee on Immigration and Naturalization in support of Japanese immigration. Throughout his testimony, Irish spoke out against what he saw as the "fury of apprehension, hatred, and rage" among leaders of the anti-Japanese movement, particularly Senator James Phelan of California.[18] Irish stood strident in his defense of the Japanese, for he had much to lose if the Japanese were to be excluded. As an agriculturalist and president of the Delta Association of California, he viewed the "Japanese as an economic necessity" noting in his defense that the Japanese were friendly and industrious people.[19] When Judge Raker asked him whether or not he believed the Japanese were assimilable, Irish pushed back. He asked the Judge to define what he meant by assimilation. "I mean a white girl marrying a Japanese young man," Raker replied. The question of Japanese assimilation into mainstream American society was, at its core, a question of interracial intimacy. Irish danced around Judge Raker's question, repeatedly stating, "that is on the knees of the gods."[20]

Some who supported Japanese immigration argued that the arrival of Japanese women in the US would prevent the mixing of Japanese bachelor men with white women. When Irish was further pressed on the question of Japanese assimilation, he answered, "I remember when Abraham Lincoln and the rest of them were advocating the abolition of slavery. All of them were supposed to be answered by the question: 'Do you want your daughter to marry a Negro?'"[21] Irish answered Judge Raker's question of Japanese assimilation with a threat disguised as a question. His answer revealed a fear of racial mixing between Japanese men and white women, even among pro-Japanese Americans like himself, a fear that underlined much of the debate about the Japanese ability to assimilate. In fact, no question came up more frequently in the hearings than the question of intermarriage between the Japanese and white Americans.[22] The question of Japanese assimilation was a euphemism masking the fear of miscegenation. Though Irish was a vocal supporter of the Japanese, he was motivated by the profit that farmers like himself made off the backs of Japanese laborers. In addition to being an outspoken opponent of Japanese exclusion, Irish was also anti-union and opposed women's suffrage. His view of immigration was largely motivated by a desire to maintain and expand his economic and political power.[23]

Irish's retort reveals the ways that Japanese men were both racialized and sexualized in the white nativist imagination. The Native Sons and Daughters of the Golden West, a leading political lobbying group calling for Japanese exclusion in California, warned that just as the South was being "negroized," so too was the West being "Japanized." "Would you like your daughter to marry a Japanese?" one member of the Native Daughters asked readers in a newsletter, for "it is not unusual these days to find, especially among the 'better classes' of Japanese, [men] casting furtive glances at our young women. They would like to marry them."[24] During the last two decades of the nineteenth century and onward, historian Peggy Pascoe explains that Asian men were pulled "steadily closer to [African American men] in the minds of American white supremacists, until they became standard companions in western miscegenation laws." While miscegenation fears focused on white women and Black men in other parts of the country, in the West that fear was aimed at

Asian men and white women. At the core of the perceived threat of Japanese men was the protection of white womanhood.[25]

In the early part of the twentieth century white settler domination in the West was not wholly complete. White male settlers openly competed with Asian male migrants—Chinese, Japanese, South Asian, and Filipino—to monopolize the labor market in an effort to "win" the West. Their battle cry cast Asian migrant men as a threat to the white way of life, which included the white man's ability to provide for his family. But the aspersions did not stop there; nativists argued that Asian male migrants were a sexual threat to white women and the American nuclear family. Whether or not Asian migrant men actually engaged in interracial intimacy with white women did not matter much. In fact, any form of kinship, intimacy, or expressed sexuality among Asian migrants in the early twentieth century—what historian Nayan Shah calls "stranger intimacies"—was believed to disrupt the racial hierarchy that white settlers were working hard to establish in the West. These "stranger intimacies" undermined the white nuclear family, the foundation for white settlement and domination. In short, Asian men were deemed a menace to the sanctity of whiteness in the West.[26]

In addition to being perceived as sexual threats to white women, Japanese immigrant men were accused of strategically replacing white women in service industry jobs. "Brown-skinned Orientals" were a menace to white working women, reported the *San Francisco Chronicle* in 1905. Japanese men were accused of deliberately taking restaurant and domestic service jobs away from white women, because the former worked for lower wages than anyone else. Once they dominated these service sector jobs, the *Chronicle* warned, they would turn around and strike for higher wages, expanding the Japanese sphere of influence. This thinking prominently displayed white American anxiety about the economic competition of Japanese male workers as well as anxiety about Japan's growing military and economic power.[27] Furthermore, Japanese men were depicted as having low hygienic standards, which posed a health threat to the restaurants they worked at and to the white Americans who patronized such establishments.[28] The article ended with a call to restrict Japanese immigration in order to protect white women from economic competition and protect white Americans, in general, from "uncleanly"

Japanese migrants. Three years later, in 1908, the Gentlemen's Agreement was made, restricting Japanese men from the laboring classes from entering the United States, yet allowing Japanese women to migrate.

The exception for wives was made, in part, because many like John Irish argued that the immigration of Japanese brides would protect white American women from Japanese men, both as lovers and economic competition.[29] Thus, the Agreement was a paradox of inclusion and exclusion drawn across gendered lines.

The Gendered Politics of the Anti-Japanese Movement

In his testimony, Irish denied a number of other accusations against the Japanese. Chief among the charges was that once Japanese women immigrated to the US, they began working in the fields, helping their husbands to cultivate crops and bearing children at a fast rate. Japanese women ostensibly entered the United States as wives to provide intimacy and companionship to their husbands, itself a form of labor. But at the core of the argument was a concern about the role their labor—reproductive and productive—would play in the farming economy and local politics on the West Coast. As such, each woman underwent an interrogation by immigration officials once she arrived to determine whether or not she was entering as a bona fide wife to a Japanese man. Such was the case of Yoshi Kiyomura.

The historiography of Japanese exclusion focuses heavily on the perceived labor, economic, and sexual threat of Japanese immigrant men in the early twentieth century.[30] Yet anxiety about Japanese women's labor and reproductive power significantly inflamed anti-Japanese discourse. Women like Yoshi Kiyomura were believed to be performing more than just "household duties." As historian Martha Gardner describes, in 1915, San Francisco immigration officials reported that Japanese women were working outside the boundaries of the home in positions that had previously been occupied by farmers or common laborers. When Japanese wives worked alongside their husbands in the fields and restaurants, they were accused of being "Japanese laborers in the guise of wives."[31] This language was explicitly drawn from "Yellow Peril" fears of a menacing Japanese invasion, though this time that fear was directed at women.

Japanese women were perceived as maliciously intending to trick white Americans into thinking they were *just* wives. Underlying this attack on Japanese women was a stubborn belief that women, especially Japanese women, belonged exclusively in the home. The logic of separate spheres ignored the fact that in many farming families across the country, women—wives, daughters, and mothers—labored on the farm in addition to their work in the home.[32]

Many of the women who entered as brides came from farming families where women's work—domestic, farming, and wage-earning—was key to sustaining the economic unit of the household and little distinction was made between domestic work and 'productive' labor. In prewar rural Japan "women in Japanese farm households were deeply involved in farm work as well as in housework, and the role [they] played, although different from the role played by men, was indispensable to the household." During the same period, women spent about equal amounts of time on farming and household work.[33] In addition to tending to family farms, young men and women, usually surplus sons and daughters, left rural Japan to work as domestics in the homes of the wealthy or in factories in urban centers while a significant portion left Japan altogether to pursue work in America.[34] In her work on Issei women and labor in Hawai'i, Kelli Nakamura found that many "were driven to become picture brides by economic factors and the promise of work." They agreed to arranged marriages as a means to "gain entry into the United States and its territories to take advantage of work opportunities."[35]

Moreover, Midge Ayukawa's study of picture brides in British Columbia, based largely on oral histories, found that with few opportunities in Japan, some women "actively chose the adventure and excitement they hoped to find in 'Amerika,' while others were motivated to immigrate to escape the subservience that would be expected of them by mothers-in-law in Japan."[36] These accounts reveal an incongruity between Japanese women's experiences, expectations, desires for self-determination, and the restrictions embedded in the Gentlemen's Agreement that circumscribed their lives in the United States.

In 1917, California congressman Everis Anson Hayes, a member of the Committee on Immigration and Naturalization, accused the Japanese of violating the Gentlemen's Agreement of 1908 because picture brides were "quite as much laborers as are the men, they go out in the fields and do the same work." Hayes's comments reveal the issue was as much about gender and labor as it was about race. The labor of Japanese women was of great concern to organized labor to the extent that the Labor Council of San Francisco took up the issue in a letter addressed to Woodrow Wilson. The Council complained to the President that the labor of Japanese women outside the home gave the Japanese an unfair advantage that displaced their white competitors.[37]

As the history of the Japanese in America shows, dynamic gendered constructions have been used to include and exclude immigrant groups. Historically those in power have used moral and sexual panics to arouse fear of "Others" who threaten the social order. In the case of the Japanese in the early twentieth century, Japanese women were targeted as birth rates among white American women declined and immigration from Japan grew. Anti-Japanese politicians feared Japanese women whose reproductive lives would shape the citizenry. Though Japanese women were denied a pathway to citizenship, their American-born children would be United States citizens. This posed a particular threat to nativists. Japanese exclusion between 1908 and 1921 was rooted in a racialized fear of Japanese women's "economic productivity" and reproductive abilities.[38] White Americans imaged Japanese women as "toylike, delicate little ladies" who nonetheless had the power to work like men and possessed the reproductive "fecundity" to give birth "as regularly and as often as [every] springtime." In so doing, Japanese women were, according to contemporary sources, orchestrating an "inside Japanese invasion of the state."[39] Anti-Japanese fears were compounded by Japan's growth as a world power since defeating the Qing Dynasty in the Sino-Japanese War in 1894–95 and the Russian Empire in the Russo-Japanese War in 1904–05.

Moreover, in the early twentieth century, a declining birth rate among white American women coupled with the influx of new immigrants arriving from southern and eastern parts of Europe and East Asia led to a fear of "race suicide" by white Americans.[40] In 1912 Myre Iseman published *Race Suicide*, a study of population patterns in the US and beyond. Iseman warned that "if the American republic is to remain Anglo Saxon and stand for the civilization of the West instead of the East, her women, particularly those of the native stock, must become its mothers."[41] *Race Suicide* popularized eugenic logic that claimed that the Teuton people, those descended from northern Europe, were the superior race and called for increased birth rates among "native stock." Iseman blamed industrialization for the declining birth rate as many white women left their homes to work in the mills or factories of industrialized America. Further, by seeking waged labor outside the home and away from the watchful eyes of authority figures, young women sought greater economic, social, and sexual independence which stoked fear in many.[42] Iseman's theories were part of a chorus of eugenicist thinking in and out of the academy that popularized and legitimated a deeply flawed view of difference.

On the West Coast, the discourse on race suicide focused heavily on the "Yellow Peril." In his call for Japanese exclusion, James Phelan, San Francisco mayor from 1897 to 1902, United States Senator from 1915 to 1921, and a prominent leader of the anti-Japanese movement, consistently pointed to the reproductive labor of Japanese women. Phelan portrayed the Japanese as invasive foreign bodies that intruded upon the nation while focusing his attack on women and children, a tactic that would become commonplace in anti-immigration campaigns in the decades to come.[43] Phelan's campaign slogan "Keep California White," conveyed a sense of urgency to stall rapid change. Including statistical data on Japanese birth rates alongside the term "aggression," Phelan implied that Japanese women's reproduction leading to the creation of Japanese American families, was an act of violence or hostility. This view of family contrasted with the logic of family ideation that undergirded the Gentlemen's Agreement. Such tactics marked a shift in the anti-Japanese movement.

In Senator Phelan's testimony before the Committee on Immigration and Naturalization, he reported the Japanese population had increased over 111 percent between 1910 and 1919.[44] Phelan's opponent, Sydney Gulick, criticized him for exaggerating statistics on the Japanese population, arguing that Japanese immigrant women were "not as efficient agents of reproduction" as Phelan claimed.[45] Phelan based much of his argument on Japanese women's "fecundity" from data derived from the Bureau of Vital Statistics of the State Board of Health. In 1920 the Board of Health reported that between 1910 and 1919, the "Japanese birth rate [in California was] far in excess of that of all other nationalities." However, the board also pointed out that high birth rates were common among "new"

Figure 1.1. An advertisement for Sen. Phelan's second bid for the senatorial seat in 1920. *Sunset, the Pacific Monthly* 45, no. 1 (July 1920).

immigrants as recent arrivals tended to be younger in age—i.e., in their childbearing years—while the white residents of California had been there longer and thus had a proportionate number of elderly citizens not of childbearing age.[46] Still, the board found that in relation to their white counterparts, Japanese women produced far more children and continued to work as farm laborers.[47] Implicit in the board's findings was the assumption that the arduous work of farming had no bearing on Japanese women's ability to reproduce and mother. This view of Japanese women contrasts sharply with that of white women portrayed by eugenicists like Iseman who believed white women were producing fewer babies because of the arduous work demanded in the mills and factories.

Phelan and other members of the anti-Japanese movement were accused of committing pogroms against the Japanese, and in previous years, against the Chinese, in their campaign to rid California of the "Yellow Peril." The pogroms were violent, resulting in death, but they were also symbolic, seeking to symbolically annihilate the Asian *other*.[48] In his defense, Phelan explained that Japanese exclusion did not amount to a pogrom. "It is not persecution; it is preservation," he argued. In other words, the exclusion of Japanese immigrants from California was an effort to preserve the white race—to "Keep California White" —as Phelan advertised in his 1920 bid for senator. Phelan and other prominent members of the anti-Japanese movement, such as the owner and editor of the *Sacramento Bee*, were successful in their campaign to exclude the Japanese. In 1921 Japan agreed to stop issuing passports to women wishing to join their husbands across the Pacific, halting the picture bride migration that had begun with the Gentlemen's Agreement.[49]

One-year prior, the *Literary Digest* published an essay drawing on translated Japanese newspapers to relate the "Japanese view of California." Several Japanese newspapers were cited at length including the Tokyo-based *Yomiuri* and *Asahi Shimbun*, and the Osaka-based *Mainichi Shimbun*, providing English readers of the *Digest* an overview of how Japanese immigration was discussed in Japan, at least according to the curators of the *Digest*. In the center of the essay is a cartoon drawn from the *Osaka Puck*, a Japanese political magazine, of a Japanese woman dressed in a kimono wearing her hair in the traditional *marumage* style.[50] She looks lovingly at the baby cradled in her arms. Behind her are rays of sunshine reflecting the Japanese imperial flag. At her foot is a white man on his knees. His name is Yankee and he is a caricature of an American politician. Underneath his right hand lays a dagger. His face is fearful, yet the dagger suggests that he is also dangerous. From the Japanese perspective the woman is a symbol of Japanese strength vis-à-vis maternal domesticity. For Americans, the image captures the pervasive fear of Japanese women's reproductive power. As contemporary political and popular discourse demonstrates, the perceived economic threat of the Japanese was profoundly influenced by fear of women's labor. To American readers, the woman was likely viewed as a Madame Butterfly. But this time she is not the idealized Asian woman of Puccini's opera or the many various cultural productions it inspired. Instead, she

FOREIGN - COMMENT

JAPANESE VIEWS OF CALIFORNIA

ANTI-JAPANESE FEELING in America is not confined to California, but prevails throughout the Union, say some Japanese editors who designate our Japanese problem on the Pacific slope as "a national issue." Tokyo dispatches relate that representative Japanese do not expect a permanent solution of the California problem until after the Presidential election. Meanwhile journals of moderate temper hope for a peaceable solution of the knotty question, and urge the Japanese people to be fair and reasonable, but firm in insisting on their rights. In newspapers of more emotional tendency we find a general condemnation of everything American, whether in the United States or in the Far East. Finally, some suggest as the only way out that the tide of Japanese emigration be turned away from the United States preferably toward South America. Among newspapers that hold this view is the Tokyo *Yomiuri*, which urges the authorities to "find a new sphere of activity for the Japanese," and adds:

"In other words, a new development of the country's colonial policy is necessary. We do not refer to the commonplace coffee plantation in Brazil, where a man can get three or four yen a day at best. The present prosperity of California is due to the labors of immigrants of a century ago. Places which bid fair to become prosperous as California in a century are legion in South America. The Japanese need not cling to a place where they are disliked. We hope that the authorities will be kind enough to try and make amends elsewhere for what the Japanese may have lost in California. It goes without saying, however, that our legitimate rights against America should be asserted to the full."

"YANKEE, WHY DOES A BIG MAN LIKE YOU FEAR MY BABY?"
—*Puck* (Osaka).

The influential Osaka *Mainichi* is one of the journals that hopes the California Japanese question will be "approached and settled in a spirit of coolness and justice," for—

"It is undesirable for either country that Japan and America should go to war over such a question. When the situation is considered from Japan's standpoint, there is ample hope that the question can be settled perfectly and in a manner consonant with justice and humanity. To be more particular, Japan should scrupulously observe the Gentlemen's Agreement, as she has done in the past, and see to it that no further emigrants are sent to America. In return for this, America should adopt no such laws as give further persecution to the Japanese already lawfully in America. The Californian agitators say that even if no further immigrants come from Japan California will be practically occupied by the Japanese. It needs no words to show that this plea has no foundation in fact. It is, however, the influx of further immigrants which is really dreaded by the Americans. We have no hesitation in urging that the cause of their alarm should be removed by refraining from forcing any further emigrants on America, for it is contrary to international etiquette to send emigrants where they are disliked."

If the Californians wish Japan to send no more emigrants and strictly observe the Gentlemen's Agreement, there is no reason, in the *Mainichi's* opinion, why Japan should not do so. Recently, it is recalled, Japan voluntarily prohibited the issue of passports to "picture brides," and when this practise, which is recognized in the Gentlemen's Agreement, is abandoned, it will be impossible for the Japanese residents in America to continue their rate of increase. But the *Mainichi* points out that—

"If American complaints relate to the increase in the number of American-born Japanese, we can only say that Japan is not concerned, for they are American citizens, and both foreigners and Japanese admit that they are more American in sentiment and manners than Japanese.

"For these reasons, if California proceeds to subject the Japanese already there to any further persecution, there will be no extenuating circumstances, and the action will be stigmatized as being entirely contrary to the principle of equity and humanity.

"The only concession which Japan can make with regard to the anti-Japanese question is strictly to observe the Gentlemen's Agreement, and to declare that she has no intention of sending any further emigrants to America. In return for this concession Japan should ask the abolition of discrimination against the Japanese already in America, including modification of the existing land-ownership law. The new law under contemplation is extremely anti-Japanese, and we should offer the strongest opposition to it."

The *Mainichi* suggests further that the Californians should consider the question quietly and should remember that—

"Many Americans admit that Japanese, whether as individuals or citizens, do not encroach on the living of Americans, and appreciate their industrious efforts in opening up the natural resources of California. As to the question of assimilation, the Americans should remember that they themselves deny the Japanese opportunities for assimilation. If the Japanese residents are neither denied the right of naturalization nor discriminated against legally and socially, they will make as good immigrants as Europeans. If the Gentlemen's Agreement, which prohibits the emigration of undesirable men from Japan to America, is strictly observed and if the Japanese Government gives an official assurance that no more emigrants will be allowed to go to America, why should the Californians impose on the Japanese injustice and humiliation such as has never been recorded in history?"

Japan is "inferior" to America in regard to wealth, it is admitted, but the history of the Japanese is "marked by too great a racial pride to allow them to brook the humiliation placed on them," and the *Mainichi* proceeds:

"Let us declare that if the Californians reject even the concessions which Japan is prepared to make and do further wrong against her people, the responsibility for the consequences shall be borne by the Californians. We propose to make a proposition which fully respects the *amour propre* of the Californians. If they violate our *amour propre*, it goes without saying that the just people of the world will not side with them. While earnestly wishing that the Californians will carefully reconsider their attitude, we hope that the Japanese Government will calmly and seriously conduct negotiations with the American Government along the lines indicated above."

The Tokyo *Yorodzu* lays all the blame for the present situa-

Figure 1.2. "Yankee, Why Does a Big Man Like You Fear My Baby?" *Literary Digest* vol. 67, 1920.

is portrayed as being under the threat of an American man. Her polite query—"why does a big man like you fear my baby?"—is meant to humiliate, to question American masculinity embodied in the white male politician's fear of a woman delicately draped in a kimono holding a helpless baby, a penetrating depiction of anti-Japanese politics.

The Specter of Prostitution

Japanese women's labor and reproductive power were not the only concerns on the minds of nativists. As many scholars have already explained, anti-prostitution campaigns in the American West disproportionately targeted immigrant women of Asian origins—first the Chinese in the late nineteenth century and then the Japanese in the early twentieth century—although their numbers were relatively low.[51] Early scholarship on Japanese prostitution in the US reveals that Japanese women were exploited at the hands of Japanese men who ran commercial sex operations.[52] In these early narratives, Issei women were mere victims of male exploitation having been deceived and sent to brothels against their will. Yuji Ichioka contends that these women were "innocent country women" duped into prostitution by male exploiters, although he notes that the lack of historical records makes it "impossible to depict the life of the prostitutes fully."[53] However, more recent scholarship tells a more nuanced story of the lives of Japanese sex workers and Japanese women in general.[54] Although some women were indeed the victims of exploitation, others turned to sex work to gain independence from men or as an economic necessity after being widowed or abandoned by their husbands.[55]

This new body of scholarship highlights the experiences of Japanese immigrant women—rather than the men who purportedly exploited them—by investigating small pockets of female agency. For instance, Kazuhiro Oharazeki argues that the boundary between working as a prostitute and working as a barmaid in the turn of the century American West was fluid. Though Japanese women indeed worked as prostitutes both involuntarily and voluntarily, they also worked as barmaids where they sometimes engaged in sex work along with the duties of maintaining the bar. Being a barmaid offered Japanese immigrant women an opportunity to engage in casual sex work to earn extra income without being confined to a brothel. The sexual encounters between Japanese men and women in brothels and bars existed as "part of a greater nexus of new possibilities between Japanese men and women, many of whom exhibited nonstandard patterns of behavior and interaction with each other upon immigration to California."[56] In other words, Japanese men and women engaged in various kinds of relationships. Within this nexus of contact, Japanese women married, divorced, ran away with, and had casual sexual relationships with Japanese men in addition to performing paid sex work. While these relationships are often described as the bad behavior of some Japanese women, evidence of complex gender relations in early Japanese American history demonstrates that Japanese women were not always and simply victims of male exploitation.

Although the number of Japanese prostitutes remained low, nativists continued to exclaim that Japanese sex workers plagued the American West, arguing that it was evidence of Japanese people's inherent immorality.[57] The specter of Japanese prostitution led the US Department of Labor to call for an extensive and systematic investigation into the occupations of Japanese women. In December 1915 the US Commissioner-General of the Department of Labor A.W. Parker wrote the commissioner of immigration in San Francisco asking him to complete an investigation into "what has become of the women and what their occupation has been since entry." Parker's probe was an attempt to weed out the "evil" that "resulted from the admission of aliens of this kind."[58] Similar to Phelan's political campaign and the anti-Japanese movement more broadly, the investigation was a project of surveillance that targeted Japanese women.

Despite their suspicions, immigration officials were unable to confirm that Japanese women were engaged in prostitution in large numbers. Inspector C. H. Hannum reported, "Japanese women, while not openly engaged in the practice of prostitution within the confines of this state, travel about in groups from ranch to ranch where Japanese men are employed, for the ostensible purpose of visiting relatives, their real mission being the practice of prostitution. This method of plyn [*sic*] their trade makes a successful investigation very difficult." Reports from the Sacramento Valley confirmed that Japanese women were working in restaurants throughout the valley and not engaged in prostitution as authorities suspected. Still, without evidence, Hannum continued to believe that the visits were a "cloak to hide their commercialized immorality."[59] One inspector commented that their efforts "to ascertain the occupations of Japanese women known as 'picture brides' have not as of yet produced definite results" indicating that officials were expected to confirm their suspicions one way or another.

The troubling case of Kiyoe Tamura Yamahata demonstrates just how far immigration officials were willing to go to locate and prosecute Japanese prostitutes. Kiyoe Tamura arrived at the San Francisco port in May 1915 at the age of twenty two. Nobutaro Yamahata, fifteen years her senior, awaited her arrival. The couple had been wed through proxy marriage; Kiyoe was arriving as Nobutaro's picture bride. Immediately after her arrival, things went downhill. The couple lived on a ranch in Suisun City where Nobutaro worked. Just two months after arriving in the US, Kiyoe became the victim of Nobutaro's violent drunken rage. One July night, a drunken Yama (as he was called by his contemporaries) attacked Kiyoe who was sick in bed. According to the closest witness, Dennie Chadbourne, owner of the ranch where the Yamahatas lived, Yama slapped, pinched, and bit Kiyoe. Dennie and his wife called on the local constable to deescalate the situation. The constable quieted Yama down and took Kiyoe home with him. He and his wife called on Donaldina Cameron of the Woman's Occidental Board of Foreign Missions of the Presbyterian Church. Cameron ran the Cameron House in San Francisco, and was a reputable woman known for her missionary work rescuing Chinese and Japanese women from prostitution, abuse, and indentured servitude.[60] Cameron took Kiyoe in, and her life started to improve. However, just two months into her stay at the Cameron house, Kiyoe became the target of an anti-prostitution investigation.

Meanwhile, Yama continued to be a problem tenant for the Chadbournes. Shortly after Kiyoe moved away, he was accused of neglecting the crops. Mrs. Chadbourne lamented to Cameron:

> I have not been to the city, could not leave the ranch this summer on account of Yama. I haven't had a vacation this summer. His Japs [referring to the Japanese farmhands Yama oversaw] tried to steal my dried fruit, so I paid my son, and another young man to watch it at night, 50 cents a night. One slept in the shed and one on dry ground. One Jap man here killed three Japs, and I said it was a shame they did not get a dozen of them.[61]

In the same letter, Chadbourne expressed empathy towards Kiyoe. "I am so glad his wife is taken care of. I feel sorry when I see her lovely trunk, and clothes with him. He is trying hard to get her back but he is dishonest." Yama's bad behavior led officials to question his background, including the steps he had taken to have Kiyoe admitted into the United States. An investigation showed that Yama had lied to immigration officials about his assets at the time of Kiyoe's arrival. With this information, immigration officials asserted that Kiyoe had entered the country fraudulently and accused her of engaging in prostitution. By their logic, Yama was a dishonest and immoral man who lied to officials about his financial status. If he was successful in lying to immigration officials about his assets, what else could he be lying about?

In reality Yama was simply a destitute farmer, an often drunk and badly behaved one. In late 1915, Cameron wrote a letter to immigration officials defending Kiyoe. During the two months that Kiyoe had been at the mission home, she was "quiet, gentle and obedient . . . a respectable innocent girl who was unfortunate enough to become the wife of a thoroughly bad Japanese." Cameron further explained, "If there is any question of either one being punished or deported, I am sure that the man is the guilty one of the two and an undesirable citizen."[62] It is unclear what happened next but by WWI Yama was with another woman named Rei (Ray). In the 1920s census, she is listed as his wife.[63] Perhaps Kiyoe left the Cameron House and started life anew. The point, however, is that Kiyoe was taken to be a prostitute simply because of her relationship to a bad man. Failing to live up to the strict code of gender propriety outlined in the Gentlemen's Agreement made Japanese women suspects. Twenty years later in 1936, Kiyoe departed for Japan. Her occupation at the time of her departure is listed as housewife. She was forty-two years old.[64]

Japanese women's potential for immorality was not only a concern for nativists but was also a primary concern among leaders within the Japanese community. As Eiichiro Azuma explains, from the early days of Japanese immigration up "until the 1920s, the question of how to control the behavior of 'the poor,' both in a moral and material sense, was among the most important agendas of the Japanese immigrant community."[65] Much of the tension was class-based as elite Japanese community members sought to control common laborers, gamblers, and prostitutes whom they deemed the "undesirable elements" of the lower classes. The reform-minded community leaders were acting out of their own sense of preservation, worried that the anti-Japanese campaigns would eventually lead to full exclusion as it had for the Chinese.[66] These leaders worked alongside reformers in Japan who were also seeking to prohibit prostitution across the Pacific in an effort to "protect the positive image of Japan as a 'civilized' country in the international community," as Kazuhiro Oharazeki has explained.[67] Japanese community reformers in the US concerned with controlling the behavior of Japanese women were informed by "Good Wife, Wise Mother" ideology (*ryōsai kenbo*), which defined a women's primary role as mother and wife in service of the family and the nation-state. This ideology, propagated by the Meiji state, took on new meaning in the United States with the arrival of picture brides.[68] For instance, Chrissy Yee Lau has shown how the Japanese Associations of America created "uplift projects" that "carved out an affective economy of respectability" concerning Japanese women in an effort to secure protections and rights in the mounting face of anti-Japanese policies.[69] Further, the compulsion to mold seemingly unruly women into respectable mothers and wives had much to do with their role in bearing the next generation.

A Difference in Views

While Japanese immigrant women were being scapegoated in anti-Japanese politics on the West Coast, another view of them proliferated throughout popular and political discourse revealing the ways gender constructions both bolstered and circumscribed notions of racial "otherness." Class status played a prominent role in American views of Japanese women. In 1926, Etsu Inagaki Sugimoto published *A Daughter of the Samurai*, a memoir detailing her life in Japan, migration as a picture bride, and life in the United States. As the title suggests, Sugimoto was from an elite family descended from the Samurai class. The memoir, written in English for an American audience, was first serialized in 1923–24 in a US magazine and was so well received that it was later published in book form. The book was successful, selling over 80 thousand copies in ten years. The book is especially remarkable as it was published just one year after the National Origins Act of 1924 restricted

Japanese immigration. Sugimoto's class status distinguished her from the Japanese immigrant women who were targeted by anti-Japanese exclusionists. According to Karen Kuo, *Daughter of a Samurai* "challenged the pervasive aestheticized and Orientalized images of Japanese women as docile, submissive Madame Butterflies and geishas." Yet many scholars assert, "Sugimoto positioned herself as the 'good' Japanese in the United States, one who was from an educated and elite (samurai) class and distinguished from 'bad' Japanese immigrants," making her an accommodationist at best.

In dispelling the racial myths of exclusionist rhetoric, supporters of the Japanese framed their arguments with an Orientalist view of Japanese women. For example, in his support of the Japanese, Irish noted that Japanese picture brides were "very, very handsome and motherly women," and noted their capacity for respectable domesticity: "The women are amiable, good wives, mothers, and housekeepers."[70] In 1917, the *Boston Globe Magazine* published an essay with the title, "Japanese women—they are very self-sacrificing because they love their husbands." The short essay did not mention the anti-Japanese campaign that was underway on the West Coast of the United States that targeted Japanese women. Instead it explained:

> It is a well-known fact that the Japanese woman makes an ideal housewife. . . . Nowhere perhaps in the world does one find a more ideal "lady" than among the wives and daughters of "fair Japonica." The Japanese wives as a rule are very modest, dutiful and, above all, perfectly faithful to their husbands.
>
> They are very devoted as well as affectionate and live up to then [*sic*] sense of duty. When they love the husband, they willingly die for him. This is not because they feel it a duty to sacrifice their lives for their husbands, but because that are so affectionate that they cannot bear to see their husbands suffering.[71]

Pro-Japanese Americans relied on gender and racial stereotypes of Japanese women drawn from *Madame Butterfly*. This view of Japanese womanhood had a long history in the West. Nearly fifty years before the Gentlemen's Agreement, American news outlets and cultural productions promoted Japanese women as "excellent wives and mothers" who were the "equal companion of man." The favorable view of Japanese women played two important functions. First, the media outlets promoting positive views of Japanese women had an interest in trade with the Pacific. They used the rhetoric of ideal womanhood to draw Japan and the US closer together in the minds of Americans. Ikuko Asaka explains that in the mid-nineteenth century, the status of women was the yardstick by which civilization was measured; the low status of women in parts of the "Orient" marked inferiority while the elevated status of women in the West indicated superiority.[72] Likening the Japanese to Americans in terms of gender relations also allowed politicians and the media to disparage the Chinese, who many saw as a growing threat to the American way of life. However, much of the idealization of Japanese femininity came from those in parts of the country that did not experience an influx of Asian migration. Referring to the post-World War II period, Historian Naoko Shibusawa explains:

> Most Westerners—with the significant exception of those in California decrying the "yellow peril"—chose to frame the Japanese in a romanticized manner, and often stubbornly refused to alter their view even after more accurate and realistic information about a modernizing Japanese became widely available.[73]

That editors at the *Boston Globe Magazine* would depict what they surely believed was a flattering image of Japanese women was not inconsequential. It reveals the strong regional nature of the anti-Japanese movement.[74] Taking "regional differences in attitudes about immigration policy" seriously, as Katherine Benton-Cohen suggests, makes clear the incongruities between federal policymakers located on the East Coast and local politics in the West.[75]

Conclusion

The Gentlemen's Agreement was meant to appease nativists in California while maintaining a friendly relationship with Japan. It was a compromise. Underlying the gendered assumptions of the agreement was that it would transform bachelor societies into respectable immigrant communities made up of heterosexual nuclear Japanese families. Japanese women would turn single Japanese men into husbands and fathers. The latter seemed less a threat. The privileging of wives in the agreement was not the first or last time the institution of marriage would trump racial exclusion for Japanese women. The family provisions made settling in the US a possibility, and with settlement came the birth of the second-generation, Nisei. While the agreement certainly excluded a large swath of men and some women from entering the US, it also ushered in a new era of women's migration. Nevertheless, the reproductive power and labor contributions of Japanese women became a source of deep tension that further fueled the anti-Japanese movement, ultimately leading to full exclusion. In response to American pressure, Japan agreed to stop issuing passports to picture brides in 1921, drastically reducing picture bride migration. Four years later the National Origins Act restricted immigration from all "Asiatic" countries.[76]

Examining Japanese women's privileged entry into the United States at a time of Asian exclusion alongside the anti-Japanese movement's attack on women reveals more clearly the ways that gender shaped Japanese inclusion and exclusion. The gendered nature of Japanese exclusion in the early twentieth century is sharply contrasted with the inclusion of Japanese war brides after World War II, demonstrating the malleability of gender and racial logic in the making of Japanese America.

2

Issei Bachelors

Unmarried Men at the Margins

[He] was not an evil man, but only an inadequate one with the most shining intentions, only one man among so many who lived from day to day as best they could, limited, restricted, by the meager gifts Fate or God had doled out to them . . .
—Hisaye Yamamoto, "Las Vegas Charley"

At noon on August 30, 1971, eighty-four-year-old Kazuyuki Araki jumped from his second story window at the All American Nursing Home in Chicago, Illinois. Two days later, his body was laid to rest. Araki was born in Japan in 1887 and immigrated to the United States in 1909, a year after the US restricted Japanese laborers—men like himself—from entering the country under the Gentlemen's Agreement of 1908. He was just twenty-two years old when he made the long trek across the Pacific. Like thousands before him, he came in search of work. In the late nineteenth and early twentieth centuries, young Japanese men, like Araki, came to the US in large numbers. Most came to advance their economic standing and planned to return to Japan after a few years of work and accumulated wealth. However, many settled along the West Coast and eventually started families after the arrival of picture brides. Others, like Araki, never returned to Japan, nor did they marry or have children in the United States. Instead, they traveled from town to town, state to state, field to farm, and railroad to fishing cannery in search of greener pastures. After arriving in the US, Araki worked various menial yet strenuous jobs. He first worked as a farmhand in Reedley, California, and after several moves along the West Coast, ended up on the sugar beet fields of northern Nebraska. Following the bombing of Pearl Harbor in December 1941, Araki, along with 120,000 other Japanese—both Japanese- and American-born—was rounded up and taken to the Heart Mountain Relocation Center in Wyoming. After the war, Araki worked as a cook in a Denver, Colorado restaurant before finally settling in Chicago.[1]

Kazuyuki Araki was born the fourth child of nine on December 24, 1887, in Tokyo. Like many young men and women, he was due to marry a neighboring woman in a traditional arranged marriage, but he longed to leave Japan and perhaps escape the yoke of tradition, while his bride-to-be wished to remain in Japan.[2] Araki evaded the arranged marriage and soon after set sail for America. After arriving at the port of San Francisco in 1909, he immediately began working as a field hand in Reedley, California, a small agricultural community twenty-two miles outside of Fresno. By the time he resettled in Chicago just after World War II, he had worked in Montana, Wyoming, Colorado, Kansas, and Missouri. He worked as a "hotel boy," store clerk, cook, domestic, and railroad hand. Later in his life when asked about his past, he boasted "that he was a hard worker and wherever he went he was liked by everybody."[3]

In his old age, Araki liked to recall the years past when he was still in contact with his family. He frequently told the story of his sister's visit to California during the 1915 Panama Pacific International Exposition in San Francisco. As the years passed, however, Araki moved further and further away—physically and metaphorically—from familial ties. Then, World War II brought destruction to his homeland, and Araki eventually lost all contact with his loved ones. Unlike Issei men who planted roots in the US by marrying and then fathering American-born children, Kazuyuki Araki had no kin in America. He did not own property, was not a citizen, and remained a Buddhist until his death.

It is unclear why Araki took his own life, but the records show that a year before his death, Araki contacted the Consulate General of Japan in Chicago and inquired about his possible return to his homeland. The consulate informed him that they were no longer issuing certificates of nationality, the document that allowed Japanese nationals without a proper passport to enter Japan, to those who held permanent residency in America, which Araki had obtained sometime prior. This left him in limbo, as he was not yet a full citizen of the US, but he also did not receive the full privileges of Japanese citizenship. In the end, Araki was alone. Only a few members of the Japanese American Service Committee and his Buddhist minister attended his funeral.

Men like Araki who remained unmarried and childless lived at the margins of Japanese American society. Compared to their counterparts who married and had families in the United States, Issei bachelors lived and died in relative obscurity. But their absence is not without consequence for it reveals the important, indeed vital, role that compulsorily heterosexual marriage and family structure played in the making of Japanese communities. For Japanese immigrant women, marriage was a mode of incorporation—albeit a highly-contested one—that facilitated their immigration to the US during a time of racial exclusion. Marriage also facilitated the settlement of Japanese American communities in the West and the emergence of the second-generation Nisei. Legacies of the women who immigrated under the Gentlemen's Agreement of 1908 and the men they married live on through their descendants. But what happens when there is no one to remember you?

Writing a gendered history of immigration does not simply mean adding women to historical accounts of migration.[4] Nor is gender synonymous with women.[5] Instead, a gendered history of migration must grapple with the "social and cultural ideals, practices, and displays of masculinity and femininity" that "facilitate or constrain both women's and men's immigration and settlement."[6] By studying the marginalized lives of unmarried Japanese immigrant men—the so-called Issei bachelors—the racialized constructions of gender and sexuality that shaped Japanese immigration to the United States and elsewhere in the Americas are made more clear. Issei bachelors were part of a larger social phenomenon that took hold in the US between 1880 and 1930. Migratory labor patterns and increased male migration spurred the growth of bachelor societies—the homosocial spaces where unmarried men lived and worked alongside one another. These bachelor communities were seen as a threat to the institutions that formed the backbone of American life. As historian Howard Chudacoff explains, "Americans have always revered and depended on the family as the chief institution for promoting citizenship and social order" and "have celebrated family life as a basic stabilizing influence in society." Therefore, those who remained outside the family were viewed as social outcasts. As a result, bachelors have been "excluded from family and social history."[7]

This chapter explores the lives of four elder Issei bachelors who resettled in Chicago after World War II to show how marriage functioned as a mode of exclusion for unmarried Japanese men. To excavate the lives of Issei men who never married, this chapter draws on the few scattered fragments of their lives that remain. In her work on the politics of archival representation, Michelle Caswell has argued that the historical existence of individuals and groups whose lives and histories have been underrepresented, misrepresented, or absent from the archives has been destroyed because representation in the archives signifies historical existence while absence means symbolic annihilation.[8] Because the vast majority of historical records of Japanese immigration to America centers on marriage, and scholarship on the history of Japanese in America has tended to focus on the family and the irrevocable disruption wartime incarceration wrought on families, the lives of those outside the sacred institution have been underrepresented, misrepresented, or worse, wholly absent. In short, Issei bachelors have been symbolically annihilated from Japanese American history. To counter the dominant historical omission of Issei bachelors, this chapter makes use of extant records held at the Japanese American Service Community (JASC), an independent community-based archive located in Chicago, Illinois. Turning to the community-based archive and away from the dominant record, as Caswell explains, offers "crucial tools for fighting the symbolic annihilation of historically marginalized groups."[9]

In 1946, a small group of concerned citizens founded the Chicago Resettlers Committee (CRC) to aide in the resettlement of nearly 20,000 incarcerated Japanese to the Chicago area. Initially, the CRC helped to resettle the large number of Issei (first-generation) and Nisei (second-generation) who left the camps to start life anew in Chicago. The CRC helped the resettled Japanese with employment, housing, and medical care. By 1954, the Committee began to shift its focus from resettlement to community service. The changes in the Committee's mission reflected the changes in the Japanese American community. As the postwar resettlement period came to a close, the services the CRC once offered to recently-incarcerated Japanese Americans were no longer needed. In 1954 the Chicago Resettlers Committee was renamed the Japanese American Service Committee to reflect its changing role within the community.[10]

By the late 1950s, the JASC began to focus heavily on the elderly Issei population, as their health and well-being became a great concern to local Japanese leaders. To this end, the JASC offered caretaking services as well as social and cultural programs to the Issei, such as home delivery meal services, adult day care, nutrition classes, English language instruction, home visitations, healthcare checkups, employment (mostly part-time jobs to keep them busy and active), arts and music programs, and seasonal festivals. The Issei remained the primary concern of the JASC until the early 70s, and the four case files used in this study come from this period. Today the JASC is committed to preserving and raising awareness of Japanese American cultural practices and history in Chicago.[11]

The elder Issei bachelors remained intimately tied to their ancestral homeland, for they were never fully incorporated into larger Japanese American communities, let alone mainstream American society. Their status as unmarried itinerant laborers from rural Japan rendered them what some elite Japanese called a "degenerated class" of "dirt peasants" and thus anathema to the assimilationist project crafted by community leaders.[12] Issei bachelors lived their lives "between two empires," neither wholly loyal to the emperor nor fully invested in America.[13] Though their status in the US was partly predetermined by their origins in predominantly poor farming families in rural Japan, their isolation was further shaped by anti-Japanese sentiment, class bias within Japanese American communities, and their unmarried status in the US. Their lives differ from the Japanese immigrant men who are more often memorialized in Japanese American history. In death, just as in life, Issei bachelors remain in the shadows. As unmarried, childless, migrant laborers, their lives have been difficult to reconstruct, and seemingly unworthy of thoughtful reflection or preservation. However, their lived experiences reveal that the traditional narrative of Japanese American history—one that favors the experiences of the elite, of families, and of their American-born children—is not the full story. The lives of these men tell us that the Japanese experience in America is far more heterogeneous than previously believed.

The lives of Issei bachelors illustrate that "the family was the key social unit for members of the prewar Japanese American community."[14] Marriage was the price of full membership, for the sacred institution was a stabilizing force that produced American-born children that tied the Issei to the United States.[15] Those elder Issei men who never married or fathered children remained outsiders in a society that already marginalized them because of racial difference.

In 1928, the American sociologist Robert E. Park published an article popularizing the theory of the marginal man. According to Park, human migration had produced a class of men who lived their lives between two diverse cultural groups and were never fully embedded into either, producing distinctive personality traits and patterns of behavior.[16] Though Park identified men of mixed racial heritage as the "paradigmatic marginal man," the marginal man need not have been of mixed-race.[17] Park describes the marginal man as a stranger who stays but never settles: "He is a potential wanderer . . . not bound as others are by local proprieties and conventions."[18] Park's analysis rests on two factors: the migration of people away from their homeland and the physical markers of racial difference. The marginal man existed because he could not culturally assimilate into the dominant American culture, for his "divergent physical traits" marked him as the "Other." In other words, racial difference made the invisible visible.

According to Park, the marginal man suffered from a low quality of life and personality deficiencies caused by his marginality. Park's theory, of course, was deeply flawed because it did not offer a critique of American racial prejudice or factor in class bias and social status among many other problems affecting the marginal man's integration into American society. Instead, for Park, the onus of marginality came from some innate deficiency among the marginalized themselves. Also missing in his analysis was any sense of community among racial minorities and immigrant groups. The marginal man may have been marginalized from mainstream American society—the "us" in Park's description of the Japanese—but may also have been fully embedded in his own ethnic enclave. Despite the limitations of Park's analysis, Issei bachelors were marginal men. They were marginalized from mainstream American society because of racial difference *and* marginalized within Japanese American communities because they were not husbands nor fathers. Further, the heteronormative mainstream forced some to live their lives on the margins because their sexual orientation or social standing.

Hideki Fukuzawa: Mobility and Circuitous Migration

In 1908 Hideki Fukuzawa left the Yokohama port aboard the Japanese cargo vessel *Kaga Maru*. He was only sixteen years old. He arrived in Seattle on May 1, 1908, just months after the Gentlemen's Agreement was finalized. Hideki—or Hugo as he was nicknamed in the US—was born in Nagata, Japan, in January 1892. Although the historical record of his life in America is slim, what does remain reveals much about the world he lived in and what mattered to him most at the end of his life. While the overall number of Japanese immigrants arriving in the United States declined in the post-Gentlemen's Agreement era, Japanese laborers continued to arrive on the shores of California and Washington state. This was in large part due to the successful work of labor-contractors in recruiting young, poor, Japanese men to work in the fields, mines, and railroads as the Chinese once had.[19] However, when Fukuzawa arrived in the United States in 1908, the labor contracting system in the Northwest was in decline, as the Gentlemen's Agreement made it difficult for those of little means to immigrate. Still, Japanese men continued to trickle in. To evade the restrictions imposed by the Gentlemen's Agreement, Fukuzawa posed as a traveling student to gain a Japanese passport and secure a spot on the *Kaga Maru*. He told authorities that he was on his way to London. His name on the official passenger list is stamped "In Transit." However, Fukuzawa never made it to London. Instead, he jumped ship and remained in the United States. In so doing, he bypassed the restrictions imposed on both sides of the Pacific, evading national policy and diplomatic agreements.

Sometime between his initial arrival date in 1908 and 1916, Fukuzawa returned to Japan. Perhaps his return to Japan was made possible with the earnings he made working on the railroads of the Rocky Mountains and agricultural fields of the Pacific Northwest. But it was likely not enough for he returned to the United States for the second time on Christmas Day of 1916; this time, however, he arrived as a coal loader aboard the SS *Tenshu Maru*. He undoubtedly took the arduous job aboard the steamship to finance his passage back to America, as the ship's arrival records indicate he had no intention of remaining in the United States. Furthermore, taking employment with an American-bound vessel meant that he could bypass immigration restrictions and gain access to America's gates once more. Officially, Fukuzawa was to remain with the SS *Tenshu Maru* and make the return trip back to Kobe where it had originally departed, but instead, he abandoned ship again.[20] In 1917 he was living and working in Seattle.[21]

By 1930 Fukuzawa had moved to Los Angeles where he worked in the kitchen of various restaurants in Little Tokyo. In Los Angeles, Fukuzawa lived as a boarder in a building that housed up to forty Japanese immigrants at once.[22] When World War II broke out, Fukuzawa was sent to the assembly center at the Santa Anita horse racetrack in Pasadena, California. From there, he was sent to the Heart Mountain Relocation Center in Cody, Wyoming. He was forty-seven years old.[23]

As the Gentlemen's Agreement ushered in a new era of settlement for many Japanese, many Issei men still remained unmarried and childless. In 1907 the United States Congress commissioned a bipartisan committee known as the Dillingham Commission to study recent immigration patterns. Conducted between 1907 and 1911, the study found that out of 1,058 "Asiatics," more than half were single, 42.1%, or 445, were married; and 1.1%, or twelve, were widowed. Of the 445 married "Asiatics," six had wives in the US while the other 439 had wives elsewhere.[24] The commission also reported that the Japanese were "for the greater part, not settlers, but migratory laborers. Furthermore, they have immigrated to the United States recently, and the expense of transportation is large compared to their wealth. For this reason they are practically unaccompanied by wives." Although the findings of the commission's report were dubious at best, there does remain some truth in their assessment of unmarried Japanese laborers.[25] By and large, Japanese immigrant men from the lower classes who conducted menial labor in the United States remained unmarried for a variety of reasons. Those who sent for a wife or returned to Japan to marry had access to resources that others like Araki or Fukuzawa apparently did not.

Unmarriable Men: Burakumin in America

In 1969, during the one hundredth anniversary celebration of the Wakamatsu colony, a pamphlet celebrating the early settlers vividly illustrated the immigration experience of the Issei. In the pamphlet, Japanese immigrants are given a collective voice that is both celebratory and melancholy. It reads: "We came to America for many reasons: because life had become intolerable where we were, because there would be no life at all unless we fled[,] . . . because something beautiful beckoned in the new land[,] . . . freedom."[26] The passage encapsulates the universality of survival inherent in the American immigrant experience at the turn of the century. It could have just as easily been read from the point of view of an Irish peasant or a displaced Mexican campesino. For Japanese immigrants, as for many others, the passage suggests that there was more at stake than the promise of wealth. Immigration to the US meant freedom when the only alternative was death. Upon their arrival, the already-marginalized Issei bachelors, many of whom came from burakumin families of the lowest social status, found themselves dismissed by middle and upper-class Japanese immigrants, adding another layer of their social isolation in the US.

Little has been written about burakumin in the United States, a lacuna largely due to a scarcity of sources and the sensitive nature of the issue. Historically, burakumin were relegated to the very bottom of the hierarchical social structure. In Tokugawa-era Japan, they were believed to be inferior subhumans who held "dishonorable occupations" that were believed to be dirty and polluting to "ordinary" Japanese. Three years after the Meiji Restoration of 1868, the Tokugawa status system was officially abolished, and burakumin were legally emancipated. However, discrimination against former burakumin and their descendants persisted—so much so that scholars of Japanese American studies have "dismissed the possibility that former outcastes emigrated [to the United States] in substantial numbers" as they lacked the resources and wherewithal essential to immigration.[27] This mode of thinking, according to Andrea Geiger, "reflect[s] the prejudice against former outcastes that still exists in some circles," including scholars of Japanese America.[28] Geiger points to the work of Yamato Ichihashi—a Nisei scholar of Japanese America—who asserted that the required sum to cover all necessary expenses was 200 yen. While this was an insignificant amount of money at the time, Ichihashi asserts that "the sum was not possessed by a member of the poorest class, nor was he able to borrow it from anybody." Besides, to travel abroad required ambition and an adventurous streak, which according to Ichihashi, the lowest classes did not possess.[29] Geiger refutes Ichihashi's statement, claiming that he had conflated character with social status and was himself a perpetuator of class inequality, for he was "deeply flawed by his own deeply entrenched class and caste biases."[30]

As one of the first scholars of Japanese descent in the United States and an early writer of the Japanese experience in America, Ichihashi's work has been essential for many historians since, and despite his biases, some current scholars continue to support his claims. However, Geiger asserts that Japanese immigrants from burakumin backgrounds very well could have migrated to the United States in large numbers at the turn of the twentieth century for two main reasons. First, the financial status of former burakumin was not always as grim as had been presented. Although many were hard hit by economic upheaval after the Meiji Restoration, some families were still able "to accumulate sufficient resources to give them access to alternatives" like emigration abroad. In addition, some were able to pull together their collective resources (perhaps that of a large family or hamlet) to send a young, able-bodied man to work abroad. Second, Geiger contends that the "baseness" of former burakumin communities has often been "exaggerated by popular prejudice."[31]

In 1952 an unpublished report written by an anonymous University of California, Los Angeles student revealed that there were former burakumin living in the United States. The student's desire to remain anonymous may reflect their own anxieties about being from a former burakumin family. The pseudonym used was Hiroshi Ito. Although rumors suggest that the report may have been one of two, no one has been able to locate the other. "Ito" found that collecting material on burakumin in the US was problematic since "there appeared to exist powerful sanctions [among Japanese Americans] against publicly identifying outcaste individuals or families." Given that no official data on former burakumin in America existed, Ito sought out informants from non-burakumin backgrounds to report on the conditions of the rumored burakumin in their communities. Most of Ito's fieldwork was conducted in Florin, California, a small town located in the Sacramento Valley where it was alleged that a large portion of the town's Japanese residents were from former burakumin families.[32] From conversations with Japanese immigrants in both Florin and Los Angeles, Ito derived specific characteristics of the burakumin in the United States. However, Ito admitted that the data collected was "extremely tentative," but as it stands, the report is the only one of its kind.[33] Though the issue of addressing burakumin life in America remains contentious today, acknowledging their possibility allows for a more robust interpretation of Japanese American history.

Kenji Nakemoto: The Possibility of Burakumin Issei

Kenji Nakemoto was born in rural Japan in the spring of 1893. He was about twenty-six years old when he arrived in Seattle in 1919. In Japan, he married a young woman and fathered one son but was separated from both mother and child when he left for America. Nakemoto's birthplace, Ehime prefecture, is located along the southern portion of the Inland Sea on the island of Shikoku. In 1966 anthropologist George DeVos and Hiroshi Wagatsuma found that historically, "outcaste communities [were] concentrated in the lands surrounding the Inland Sea, the ancient heartland of early Japanese culture."[34] Furthermore, the 1920s Japanese census revealed that Ehime was home to 494 burakumin communities—the largest population out of the forty-two prefectures listed—while Fukuoka and Hiroshima prefectures contained 493 and 406 respectively.[35] That Nakemoto came from a prefecture known for its abundant burakumin communities is significant. His status in Japan undoubtedly influenced his decision to leave. Perhaps he sought to escape the burden of his ancestral lineage, for "emigration to the North American West offered a way to avoid caste-based discrimination because in North America, one need only identify oneself as a Japanese subject." [36] Immigration to America, therefore, gave Japanese men from former burakumin families the opportunity to shed their status. In America, they were not burakumin, but Japanese.

When he arrived in the US, Nakemoto had plans to work, save money, and return home to buy land. Yet somehow along the way his plans diverged. Some years after his arrival in Seattle, Nakemoto found his way to California. In 1930 he was working as an asparagus picker in the small town of Clarksburg located along the Sacramento River.[37] The latitudinal positions of Clarksburg and Nakemoto's homeland, Ehime prefecture, are nearly identical. On a map, a straight line can be drawn connecting the two. Whether Nakemoto realized the connection between his ancestral homeland and the asparagus fields of northern

California remains a mystery. That he chose to leave Seattle and head south speaks to the frequent movement of Issei bachelors. Most traveled throughout the western United States in the years before World War II seeking out the next great lead that would facilitate their triumphant return home. Surely Nakemoto was lured by the call of the Golden State after the perpetual rain and chill of Seattle. He must have found it hard to resist the clear blue skies, year-round sunshine, and abundant employment opportunities for men like him.

In California, Nakemoto found himself surrounded by other Japanese. He probably worked alongside other men from rural Japan—men accustomed to arduous work in the fields. More than likely he was supervised by a Japanese "boss" who acted as a middleman between field hands and growers. Or perhaps he worked for a Japanese-owned operation. Besides his fellow countrymen, Nakemoto may have also worked with men from Mexico and the Philippines as well. In 1930 there were nearly 56,000 Filipinos living on the West Coast, and they comprised "80 percent of the asparagus workforce in the Sacramento River Delta region."[38] Perhaps Nakemoto befriended Filipino field workers. Perhaps there was tension between the two groups. But more than likely, there was both friendship and conflict in the California asparagus fields.[39]

In 1924, five years after Nakemoto arrived in the United States, Congress passed the National Origins Act which severely limited the immigration of "racially undesirables." The act notoriously restricted all Asian persons from entering the country.[40] The Japanese had been excluded from naturalizing per the 1790 Naturalization Act which allowed only "free whites" to naturalize, and now they were excluded from American shores.[41]

Until 1924, returning to Japan took one of two forms. First, if one returned to Japan, the possibility that he could come back to the US was conceivable. Although the immigration process had become increasingly exclusive, one could, as in the case of Hideki Fukuzawa, evade such restrictions. Therefore, circulatory migration was feasible, if difficult to manage.[42] The other option was to return to Japan permanently, as many did. However, after the closing of America's gates in 1924, the options available to Japanese laborers in America became extremely limited. Historian Mae Ngai explains, "Japanese immigrants felt thoroughly dejected by the 1924 immigration act, which foredoomed them to permanent disfranchisement and social subordination. Their only hope lay in the Nisei [their American-born children], the second-generation."[43] But those without children would have to look elsewhere. With no children to carry their legacy, Issei bachelors had to invest their hope into the thought of returning home someday.

By the outbreak of World War II, Kenji Nakemoto had moved on to Stockton in the San Joaquin Valley, about fifty miles from Clarksburg. One imagines that he may have worked for various growers in and around California's Central Valley, as did so many Issei bachelors. He never re-married nor had children in the US and remained a faithful Buddhist. Nakemoto may have felt a sense of home and belonging in the fields among others like him, or perhaps he felt alienated by the laborious work and lack of kinship. Regardless, he gave the remainder of his youth to the California fields. In the spring of 1942 when the order went out to all Japanese living on the West Coast to pack their bags and head to the nearest assembly center, Nakemoto was forty-nine years old. Later, he was moved to the Minidoka camp in Idaho. In the summer of 1945 at the end of the war, he boarded a train headed for Chicago.

Sexuality and the Case of Jiro Onuma and Yone Noguchi

While some Issei men remained bachelors because of racial prejudice, class and social status bias, and the demands of low-wage work that prevented them from marrying, queer men like Jiro Onuma chose not to marry. These men rejected the heterosexual institution of marriage. As such, their experiences have also been grossly underrepresented or completely absent from history. However, a small but growing body of research has emerged aiming to correct this historical omission. Like the Issei men who remained unmarried or those from the former outcaste society, queer Japanese men were outsiders. In exploring their lives, a more varied image of Japanese America emerges. These alternative histories demonstrate how marriage and family functioned as the primary locus of inclusion and belonging in Japanese American communities. At the same time, they highlight how the lack thereof meant exclusion for many.

Onuma entered the United States in 1923, fifteen years after the Gentlemen's Agreement of 1908 and just a year before the National Origins

Act would restrict all Japanese immigration. Settling in San Francisco and working as a launderer and then a butler, Onuma was one of a very few openly gay Issei men. Onuma's personal archive is held at the Gay, Lesbian, Bisexual, Transgender Historical Society in San Francisco.[44] The bulk of the slim archive consists of photographs of young Japanese men and other "homoerotic ephemera," mainly a collection of "male physique magazines."[45] In the photographs, the young men (including Onuma) are well-dressed and smiling. Women are completely absent except for a few photos of Onuma traveling abroad later in life with friends—a married heterosexual couple. Though little is known about the men in the photographs, the plethora of photos in Onuma's possession, totaling over one hundred, reveals that he had many male companions. That Onuma resided in an area with many bachelor hotels indicates that he was part of a thriving if clandestine gay subculture of Japanese men in prewar San Francisco. In other words, Onuma was not alone.

Yone Noguchi was born in 1875 and immigrated to the US in 1893 at the age of eighteen. Upon arriving in the US, Noguchi worked various low-paid, menial jobs but would eventually become a well-known poet and writer as well as the father of famed Japanese American sculptor Isamu Noguchi. Though Noguchi engaged in heterosexual relationships including marriage, he also became romantically involved with men. Indeed, Noguchi led a tumultuous love life, finding himself in the middle of a queer-straight love triangle. At one point, Noguchi carried on affairs with two women: Leonie Gilmour, with whom he fathered a child, and Ethel Armes, both well-educated, white American women, and Charles Warren Stoddard, a man his senior.[46] Noguchi's and Onuma's lives and the queer intimacies they sought illustrate the varied lives of Issei men—a history marked by racism, class bias, and in some cases, sexual orientation.

"Nasty" Men and "Ignorant Farmers": Issei Bachelors in Wartime Incarceration Camps

After the Japanese attack on Pearl Harbor on December 7, 1941, racial hysteria swept the country. Soon after, President Franklin Delano Roosevelt issued Executive Order 9066 ordering all persons of Japanese ancestry living along the West Coast to evacuate at once and report to an official assembly center. They were only allowed to bring what they could carry. The devastation wrought by World War II was catastrophic for the Japanese in America. For many Japanese laborers who immigrated to America at the turn of the century, it was the beginning of the end. Their best years were behind them, and the hope that they would someday return to Japan in triumph was nearly lost. It is unclear what assembly center Kenji Nakemoto reported to, but there were fourteen in the state of California—one located at the San Joaquin County Fairgrounds in Stockton where Nakemoto was living and working.

Many Issei men and women who had carved out a modest yet fulfilling standard of living had to leave behind their personal belongings—homes, cars, furniture, and clothing. Many left behind businesses, friends, lovers, and pets. But Issei bachelors had very little to leave behind. All their worldly possessions could be carried on their backs. Although their forced incarceration was undoubtedly disruptive, in some ways it was just another move in a long life on the road. For Issei bachelors with little to their name, the experience of wartime incarceration was undoubtedly different than their married counterparts. World War II incarceration was one in a sequence of difficulties. While much has been written about married Issei and the Nisei experience in wartime incarceration camps, relatively little is known about the experiences of Issei bachelors.

In the fall of 1942, Kenji Nakemoto was relocated from an assembly center, presumably the Stockton Assembly Center at the San Joaquin County Fairgrounds, to the Minidoka Relocation Center located in Jerome County, Idaho. During its three-year operation from September 1942 to October 1945, Minidoka was home to 13,078 people of Japanese descent—Kenji Nakemoto included.[47]

James Sakoda was also incarcerated at the Minidoka camp. As a university student during the war, Sakoda, a Nisei, worked as a research assistant in Minidoka on behalf of the Japanese American Evacuation and Resettlement Study (JERS) directed by University of California, Berkeley sociologist Dorothy Swaine Thomas. The goal of JERS was to collect data on the "enforced migration" of Japanese Americans to ultimately aid officials in dealing with dislocated populations in postwar Europe.[48] Under the aegis of JERS, Sakoda (along with several other

Nisei university students) collected data on his Japanese brethren in the camps and kept a personal diary of his encounters and thoughts about the war, incarceration, and the status of the Japanese in America more broadly. Sakoda and others had a precarious position as insider and outsider, participant and observer. The data collected for JERS and its subsequent publications, *The Spoilage* (1946), *The Salvage* (1952), and *Prejudice, War, and the Constitution* (1954) imparts some understanding of the differences in the lived experiences of the incarcerated Japanese. Of notable interest is Sakoda's description of the Issei bachelor population.[49]

While in Minidoka, James Sakoda observed that the Issei population had self-segregated along class lines. He remarked:

> People who were generally successful held themselves above the so-called immigrant group. They felt that they [the immigrant, non-assimilated group] were not being sophisticated. Sometimes they called them ignorant farmers; they [the successful Issei] had that kind of attitude.[50]

Sakoda further found that those from the lower classes—the "ignorant farmers"—were not loyal to the United States. Since the Issei bachelors had no families, they showed little investment in America. Instead, they cheered for Japan to win the war, spread rumors of America's defeat, and balked about having to fill out the "loyalty questionnaire."[51] Sakoda recalled:

> They were frustrated and they didn't have any property; they didn't have children to worry about so they would say, "Don't register. We're going back to Japan. Japan's winning the war." They circulated a lot of rumors of Japan winning the war. "They're going to reward us with $10,000 and they're going to take us on a tour of the South Sea Islands." That sort of rumor circulated among the Issei men.[52]

Sakoda's remark reveals the disappointment felt by the dispossessed Issei. In theory, nothing kept them from staying in the United States. With no wife or children in the US and no hope for a successful or lucrative job to facilitate their return home, there seemed no reason for the propertyless, single Issei men to stay or show loyalty to the United

States. In reality, however, returning to Japan was a less viable option after the war. The latter half of Sakoda's remark, referring to a rumored $10,000 reward and tour of the South Sea Islands, either seems a fanciful idea about postwar reconciliation or reveals a perceptive sense of humor among some of the Issei bachelors in Minidoka. Still, according to Sakoda, the Issei bachelors were a "sorry lot" because they were not able to obtain wives from Japan, "did not have the financial means to enjoy life," and had no "children to provide integration with the American community."[53]

Sakoda's disdain for the Issei bachelors he observed was shaped by his own class bias, for the Sakoda family had reached a level of success that distanced them from the struggling Issei. But equally important, Sakoda was a "loyal" Japanese who answered, "yes-yes" on the loyalty questionnaire. During the war, the War Relocation Authority (WRA) mandated that the incarcerated Japanese take a compulsory loyalty test to prove their allegiance to the United States. Questions number 27 and 28 were especially contentious and confusing. Question 27 asked men of military age if they were willing to serve in the US Armed Forces, and question 28 asked every incarcerated individual if they were willing to swear allegiance to the United States and renounce loyalty to the Japanese emperor. As Mae Ngai has shown, the loyalty questionnaire was a source of tension among the incarcerated Japanese since many were influenced by a sense of dual nationalism—they were loyal to the US but also culturally tied to Japan. Ngai explains, "They held complicated, divided loyalties, a set of allegiances that sustained commitment to life in America alongside affective and cultural ties, even patriotic sympathies, with Japan."[54] By answering yes to the question of loyalty and working as a researcher for JERS, Sakoda had aligned himself with the US while many Issei bachelors expressed pro-Japanese views.[55] Sakoda's remarks suggest he was ideologically opposed to their musings about the war. The Issei bachelors, then, were more politically aligned with the "No-No Boys," a group of young Japanese men who answered "no" to questions 27 and 28 of the loyalty questionnaire in protest of their forced incarceration. Sakoda was not alone in his disdain for disloyal Issei bachelors. One young Japanese woman who worked for the Army registration called Issei bachelors "nasty" and part of "one of the worst blocks" in camp. "They were crude and uncouth, and they made fun of me when I tried to reason with them," she lamented. Of course, by "reason with them," she meant she was trying to persuade them to answer yes on the loyalty questionnaire.[56]

In addition, the WRA had organized the incarcerated by family unit, ensuring that single Issei men would remain separated from the rest of the population. In short, Issei bachelors were doubly marginalized. And yet, the all-male units created a homosocial world not unlike the camps in the agricultural fields and along the railroads where poor Japanese men labored. The camps "afforded unique opportunities to resourceful queer men" to engage in same-sex intimacy.[57] In fact, in Jiro Onuma's possession is a photograph taken in camp of himself, his lover Ronald, and another male friend. The photo suggests that same sex intimacy indeed took place in the camps.[58] Much has been written about the disruption World War II incarceration had on family life. But for marginalized Issei men who did not have families of their own, the experience of wartime incarceration differed.

Issei bachelors had no economic or familial stake in the United States and perhaps, because of this, were apt to sympathize with Japan. Some openly expressed their dissatisfaction with the US and looked toward their homeland for redemption. In camp, they tended to be the "disgruntled, dissident group."[59] Yet, little mention of the camps can be found in the JASC records of Kenji Nakemoto, Hideki Fukuzawa, or Kazuyuki Araki. Their World War II incarceration is only mentioned in passing and no details are given; of course, the records are limited in scope and depth. The war, however, strained their independent sensibility and severed the familial ties that bound them to Japan. The utter devastation of the war meant that contact was lost between the Issei in America and their relatives in war-torn Japan. It would take some nearly two decades to reestablish contact with their loved ones across the Pacific.

The mundanity of wartime incarceration experienced by single Issei men was also expressed in Japanese American fiction. In Hisaye Yamamoto's short story, "Las Vegas Charley," a lonely widower named Kazuyuki Matsumoto (later known as Charley) is described as feeling content in camp: "Free food, free housing, friends, flower cards [Charley's favorite pastime]; what more could life offer?" In addition, Charley received free medical treatment for his hearing loss in one ear. Charley had, at one point in his life, a farm, a wife, and two sons. But Charley lost his wife after the birth of their second son, and then years later lost his first son in the war. The story of Charley illuminates the disappointment and despair that led some Issei men without families to embrace camp life. When, in the short story, another Issei man curses the US for stealing his farm and making him suffer, Charley quietly disagrees.[60]

In 1943 the WRA began to aggressively promote relocation of all Japanese held in the incarceration camps to the Midwest and other parts of the country away from the West. Nearly 20,000 incarcerated Japanese relocated to Chicago at the war's end. Kenji Nakemoto, Hideki Fukuzawa, and Kazuyuki Araki were part of this mass, forced migration to the Windy City. In Chicago, they found housing difficult to secure. Most Japanese newcomers to the city found that the only options available to them were hostels, boarding houses, or tenement-style living located in three main parts of the city. Issei bachelors resettled largely in the North Loop area, where "rundown rooming houses, hotels, and a large number of cheap night clubs and bars" could be found, while others settled on the city's southside.[61] Work was plentiful, although the nature of it had changed.

After spending nearly three years in Minidoka, Kenji Nakemoto applied for clearance to leave the camp in the summer of 1945. He arrived in Chicago shortly thereafter and began working as a cook in a downtown restaurant. He took residence in a boarding house just north of the Loop. Later, he recalled that before heading to California he had worked as a cook in the Pacific Northwest. In Chicago, he returned to this familiar work in the kitchen. His days of toil in the warm California sun were over. No longer would he work in the agricultural fields and farms of the West. In Chicago, he eked out a modest existence, but as the days went on, life seemed to grow harder to bear for Nakemoto, and he turned to drinking.

Matsuhiro Daiko: Reestablishing Contact with Japan

On May 27, 1965, Matsuhiro Daiko walked into the Japanese American Service Committee smelling of alcohol. He told staff members that he "needed immediate assistance for food and rent." A worker gave him ten dollars. He left and returned six days later asking for further financial assistance. This time, however, the worker explained to Daiko that the committee could not simply hand out cash to those in need as they had on his first visit. Instead, the worker offered him the social services available through the committee, which he accepted. On June 21, Daiko asked the worker to visit him at his apartment on Montrose Avenue in Chicago's Uptown neighborhood. When the worker arrived, Daiko lay ill. He complained of pain in his legs and hip. He asked the worker to phone the doctor; two days later he was hospitalized.

On August 2, 1965, just two months after he first showed up at the JASC office smelling of liquor and in need of help, Matsuhiro Daiko passed away. In his possession were a few household items: letters, old clothes, an electric shaver, and a phonograph, which he was still making payments on. All the items were disposed of by a social worker, while his phonograph was returned to the Tri-Par Radio Company. His body was sent to the Matsumoto Funeral Home, one of the only funeral parlors in the city servicing the Japanese community.

Little is known about Daiko's immigration and early days in the United States. He was born on November 24, 1902, in Fukuoka, Japan, and immigrated to the US around 1920. Daiko's life was marked with a tragic sense of disappointment. More than likely, he immigrated to the US to work and save. But, like the others, his plans eventually unraveled. He never married nor had children and found himself in trouble with the law on at least one occasion. On July 1, 1954, Daiko wrote a letter to Kenji Nakane, the director of the JASC, from the Chicago House of Correction thanking Nakane for "taking care of [his] matters." Nakane had interceded on Daiko's behalf, seeing to it that his room and belongings remained intact while Daiko served a sentence at the House of Correction.

A few years before his brush with the law, Daiko established contact with a niece in Japan.[62] The two exchanged letters for some time, but it is unclear if they remained in contact at the time of his death in 1965. In the spring of 1951 Nobuko Daiko wrote:

> With the arrival of the beautiful spring, I received your letter happily. I am Daiko Nobuko, Uncle. It's finally our first time to talk to each other. I am imagining how you are in various ways. I have not seen you, Uncle, and it is my first time that I read your letter, so I don't know anything about you. But my good father and mother always rumored about you. I

> don't know how you are, but I imagine that you are a kind person. Yes, I believe you are a good person.

Although Matsuhiro Daiko lived most of his life in the United States, he was never forgotten in Japan. His immigration became something of a family legend, his brother keeping his image alive in his absence. Nobuko continued to speak nostalgically of her own father, Matsuhiro's brother, who had died three years earlier. She lamented, "If my father were alive, he would be so happy. Only if I received this happy letter sooner, but we can't help [that now]." She went on to praise her uncle for having taken the risk of moving abroad and living out his "strong dream" to live in the United States. She also expressed excitement over Daiko's relationship with a "Spanish" woman named Maria, though no other evidence of this relationship exists. Still, this suggests that Daiko was at some point involved with a non-Japanese woman, presumably someone of Mexican or Puerto Rican descent. She concluded by congratulating Matsuhiro for his accomplishments:

> You must have gone through difficulties after moving to the U.S. at such a young age. But I heard that you fully explored and lived your life, given by God, and you don't feel any inconveniences now. You completely deserve it. You have received blessings from God.

Nobuko Daiko's letter conveys little awareness of the loneliness and isolation Matsuhiro seemingly felt at the end of his life. Instead, it is shrouded in valor. It seems that Nobuko may have been misled about the supposed "inconveniences"—or lack thereof—in her uncle's life. Matsuhiro Daiko must have wanted it this way.

The Last Days

After resettling in Chicago in 1945, Kenji Nakemoto worked at various restaurants and hotels, but by 1962 he had "retired" and began working instead at the JASC work center, to keep his mind busy and his days occupied. He can be seen in photograph accompanying the August 1965 *Chicago Tribune* article entitled, "A New Way of Life for Elderly Japanese Americans." In the image, he is assembling the handle of a fishing pole in the work center.[63] In 1969 a caseworker from the JASC visited him in his room to check on his wellbeing and discovered that Nakemoto had been drinking excessively and crying. She noticed that his face was red, and he appeared to be wiping tears from his eyes. What troubled Nakemoto was not made clear in the report.

In October 1962 it was reported that Nakemoto arrived at the work center "with his guard up" but eventually appeared more relaxed. A year later, however, he "feigned illness for two months" to get out of work. His coworkers, other elderly Issei, told JASC officials that he had not been ill as he had claimed. Then on June 11, 1963, Nakemoto showed up to work "staggering drunk" and rudely obnoxious: "He went down the line greeting everyone with a wave and a whack on the back missing only the supervisor."[64] He was escorted out of the building. A week later he returned "looking very sheepish" but was not dismissed because he was known to be a hard and diligent worker. Over the next few years, Nakemoto waxed and waned between "lost weekends" of isolation and binge drinking and working hard while earning praise at the work center. In August 1964 it was reported, "Mr. Nakemoto continues to be one of the fastest male workers. His only fault is that every 6 to 8 months he goes on a 'lost weekend' and is out for a week to 10 days and then returns to steady productive work again."

During his turbulent last days, Kenji Nakemoto re-established contact with his younger sister, Yukie, now living in Matsuyama City, Ehime. In March 1962 she wrote:

> I am so glad to hear that you are doing well. We are also well (so please don't worry about us). I am already old. I have seven healthy children and one who died in the war. . . . As you probably know already, it's been about 15 years since Mother died.

Nakemoto presumably had little to no contact with his family in Japan even before the war, given that Yukie made a point to introduce him to her children, noting that the eldest was a son of forty-seven years. In the same letter, she continued by filling Nakemoto in on life in postwar Japan:

> Japan, too, has surely changed after the war. We, farmers, live a cultured life nowadays and we have electric appliances at home—TV, sewing

> machine, washing machine, electric heater, and rice cooker. . . . Land situation has also changed. Most of the area I live, the county with many hot springs, was amalgamated into Matsuyama City. Kume Village was merged into Matsuyama city four or five years ago, and Ono Village last year. . . .

Yukie's words speak to the sweeping changes in Japanese life in the aftermath of World War II. Moreover, she conveys a sense of yearning to be reunited with her long-lost brother. She recounts the story of Mr. Katsuichi, a young man presumably from their village, who immigrated to Peru around the same time Nakemoto left for America. After

Figure 2.1. Young Kenji Nakemoto. Group 8, series 3, box 1, folder 50. Japanese American Service Committee Legacy Center, Chicago, IL.

Figure 2.2. Photo of older Kenji Nakemoto. Group 8, series 3, box 1, folder 50. Japanese American Service Committee Legacy Center, Chicago, IL.

Mr. Katsuichi died in Peru, his adult son returned to Japan to settle. Yukie then asks, "Why don't you come back, too, brother, one day? I took a photo of me the other day, but it does not look good, so I will take another one soon and send it to you next time." She ends the letter, "Please send your recent photo if you have one. . . . Take care of yourself . . . Yukie." A few years later Kenji Nakemoto died of pneumonia exacerbated by severe liver damage. Before his death, Nakemoto told his caseworker that he had come to America to earn money and had planned to return to Japan to buy land. In his last days, he was still hopeful that he would return to Japan to live out the remainder of his life.[65] In his possession were several photos of himself and Yukie's letters.

In 1973 when Hideki Fukuzawa was eighty-one years old, he wrote to distant relatives in Japan expressing his dying wish to return home. The following spring, Fukuzawa boarded a plane with a tour group headed to Japan. After spending most of his life in a foreign land, he finally returned home. He had first arrived in the US by steam ship in 1908 and again in 1917; when he returned to Japan in 1973, sixty-five years after his initial arrival, he did so by plane.[66]

Once he arrived in Japan, Hideki Fukuzawa wrote to his caseworker at the JASC: "Japanese people are polite and kind. I haven't seen them for 65 years, but they treat me so nicely as if their sibling came back." After spending a lifetime away, Japan was foreign to him. To his surprise, "They also rebuilt an American style apartment (with parlor, bedroom, kitchen, and bathroom), and I sometimes get confused where I am—in Japan or the U.S." He continued, "After I arrived in Japan, I visited Tokyo, Kyoto, Nara, Shikoku, Osaka—the 'heart' of Japan, with a group, and arrived finally in my hometown [Arai-shi, Niigata]." Hideki had become a tourist in his own country, and after spending decades away; he was reacquainting himself with Japan. In February of 1974, just months after he returned to Japan, Hideki Fukuzawa passed away. He was eighty-two years old.[67]

Conclusion

When Japanese immigrant men began arriving on the shores of the western United States they did so with dreams of financial security. Many from the farming class—and likely from former burakumin families—planned to work, save money, and return to Japan in triumph. But the closing of America's gates, interethnic class divisions, and racial persecution severely limited their chances of returning home or finding prosperity in America. When the Japanese military attacked Pearl Harbor on December 7, 1941, their fate was sealed. Wartime incarceration and the devastation of Japan severed the ties that once bound many to their homeland in the prewar period. Some were able to reestablish connections with loved ones after the war, but by then, they were strangers in their homeland. For those Issei men who did not marry or father American-born children, full membership in Japanese America lay beyond their reach. When Kazuyuki Araki took his life in 1971 at the age of 84, he was alone in a rapidly-changing city and unable to return to Japan. Perhaps this was his coup de grâce.

The absence of marriage and a nuclear family resulted in the exclusion of the Issei bachelors, but for Japanese women, marriage and family were the means of conditional inclusion. In the aftermath of World War II Japanese women arrived on US soil to join their husbands, just as their predecessors did between 1908 and 1924. This time, however, they arrived as wives and fiancés of American men in uniform. The migration of Japanese war brides was made possible by legislation that favored normative nuclear family structures. Their arrival signaled a change in US-Japan relations, a change that was neither wholly welcomed nor rejected.

3

The US Occupation of Japan and the Making of Postwar Japanese America

The alien spouse of an American citizen by a marriage occurring before thirty days after the enactment of this Act, shall not be considered as inadmissible because of race, if otherwise admissible under this Act.
—Public Law 271, 80th US Congress, July 22, 1947

Setsuko Williams was born in Nagoya, Japan, in July of 1926. She was the oldest of ten children from a middle-class family and lived her early childhood years in comfort. Her father worked for the Imperial Japanese Government, making what she called a "pretty good living," while her mother took care of the children and home. However, Setsuko's days of childhood comfort were numbered. In 1937, when she was just eleven years old, total war broke out between Japan and China in the Second Sino-Japanese War. Setsuko's father was conscripted to fight in the Imperial Japanese Army. He returned home after the war alive and well, but for Setsuko, war had become an integral part of her early life.[1]

When Japan entered World War II in 1939, Setsuko was just thirteen years old. During the war she joined her mother in caring for the family. Then, at the height of the war, seventeen-year-old Setsuko married a young Japanese man in a traditional arranged marriage. Three months after their wedding in July 1943, he was sent to serve in the Imperial Japanese Army in the Pacific and never returned. By the time of the Japanese defeat in 1945, Setsuko was a nineteen-year-old widow. She took a job as a typist for the United States military at Camp Gifu during the Allied Occupation. As a Japanese civilian working for the Allied Forces, Setsuko was able to obtain some stability in the midst of economic deprivation.[2] At Camp Gifu, she met her second husband. Eddie Williams was an African American serviceman with the all-Black Twenty-Fourth Infantry Regiment. Every day when Setsuko and her coworkers took a break from work, they passed the mess hall where Eddie worked. The two exchanged glances over time, and on one rainy day after work, he offered her a ride and she accepted. Although there was no official ban on "fraternization" between American GIs and Japanese women, unofficial policy strictly prohibited contact between Japanese civilian workers and American servicemen.[3] Despite this, Setsuko and many other Japanese women like her socialized with, courted, and eventually married American servicemen. At Camp Gifu a high proportion of these relationships were between Black servicemen and Japanese women.

Racial tensions in Occupied Japan and the interracial intimacies between American GIs and Japanese women that emerged in the aftermath of World War II shaped the postwar making of Japanese America. When the war in the Pacific ended on September 2, 1945, the US sent thousands of military troops to Japan to dismantle the armed forces and democratize the Imperial Government in what is formally known as the Allied Occupation of Japan.[4] During the occupation and the subsequent Korean War, an estimated 450,000 American servicemen and women served in Japan. This analysis broadens the chronological scope to include the US military presence in Japan during the Korean conflict, since thousands of American military troops were shuffled between Korea and Japan during the Korean War between 1950–53.[5] During this historic period, American servicemen of all racial and ethnic backgrounds engaged in a range of intimate relationships with Japanese women. The briefest relationships took place in brothels where women referred to as "Panpan" girls engaged in sex work with the servicemen.[6] In some cases, the woman would have only one customer who would come to visit her on a regular basis.[7] In addition, Japanese women and American GIs engaged in courtships that led to marriage. These couples met in dancehalls and restaurants. Others met under more banal circumstances: at work for the occupation forces or through mutual friends. These men and women came together in natural ways in an otherwise unnatural environment shaped by war, military occupation, and American racial politics.[8] Many of these relationships would ultimately lead to a new wave of Japanese immigration to the US.

Occupied Japan was a liminal space between the US and Japan—enemy and ally, conqueror and conquered. Like Hawai'i and other Asian Pacific islands with a large US presence, Occupied Japan was "a highly charged arena in which the individual dramas of cultural contact played out."[9] At the center of this historic moment of contact were ordinary Japanese and American people whose daily interactions helped to reshape relations between the two recently warring nations. Above all, the intimate relationships between American servicemen of all racial backgrounds and Japanese women helped shape postwar immigration to the United States, contributing to the making of Japanese America.

Three key developments arose in the United States as a result of these interracial relationships. First, the intimacy between American servicemen of all racial backgrounds and Japanese women contributed to the making of a mixed-race post-World War II Japanese America. Once in America these Japanese women and their families were never integrated into Japanese American communities and have since not been fully included in the historiography of Japanese America.

Second, the interracial intimacies between American GIs and Japanese women abroad shaped postwar immigration legislation.[10] In the early postwar era, Japanese women were barred from entering the US per the National Origins Act of 1924, which set an immigration quota for each sending country. The quota system favored northern and western European countries and limited migration from the southern and eastern parts of Europe. The act excluded people from Asian countries altogether. Under the Origins Act, the Japanese were ineligible for citizenship based on a presumption that they, like other Asian nationals, were unable to assimilate into the dominant American culture. As historian Mae Ngai explains, the National Origins Act constructed racial hierarchies based on the "desirability" of certain immigrant groups, a "desirability" rooted in the belief that "the United States was, and should remain, a white nation descended from Europe."[11]

In an attempt to appease white American soldiers stationed throughout Europe who wished to bring their European war brides home to the States, the US passed the GI Brides Act in 1945. The act was created "to expedite the admission to the United States of alien spouses and alien minor children of citizen members of the United States Armed Forces."[12] However, the act explicitly barred alien spouses deemed "racially ineligible" by the 1924 Origins Act. Under the GI Brides Act of 1945, Japanese women were still prohibited from entering the country. Pressured by heartbroken American servicemen and civil rights groups like the National Association for the Advancement of Colored People (NAACP), the Japanese American Citizens League (JACL), and the American Civil Liberties Union (ACLU), Congress expanded the GI Brides Act of 1945 to include Asian brides of US servicemen. In 1947 the Alien Brides Act was passed permitting "alien spouses," otherwise deemed "racially ineligible," entry into the United States. However, the act stipulated that the couples had to marry and apply for immigration to the US within a thirty-day timeframe, and for many, this was impossible. Still, some managed to marry even under such restrictive terms. Those who did not meet the deadline would have to wait until August 1950 when the window to marry and apply for immigration was extended to March 1952, the year that also marked the official end of the National Origins Act.[13] Thus, Japanese women were eventually granted entry. These women were part of a larger trend in US immigration policy that privileged wives in times of racial exclusion.[14]

Those who supported expanding immigration policy to include war brides viewed such legislation as a reward for the men who served the United States military during the war. It was "the least we can do for the men who fought our wars overseas," explained Noah Mason, a US representative from Illinois.[15] Yet the privilege of bringing home wives from abroad applied mostly to white American servicemen. African American servicemen, on the other hand, faced additional obstacles in securing immigration for their brides.

Finally, the interracial encounters in Occupied Japan shaped ideas about civil rights in the post-World War II United States. World War II marked a shift in the ways in which Black Americans understood the stakes of interracial intimacies in civil rights discourse, and many Black servicemen involved with Japanese women expressed solidarity with the Japanese. In the post-World War II era, "Black GI interracial intimacy signified the most public form of Black activism centered on interracial intimacy and marriage."[16] This activism was made visible by a "burgeoning Black public culture" in addition to lobbying by Black men.[17] Yet the connection between racial equality and interracial intimacies privileged heterosexual male desire.

Marriage served as the primary mode of inclusion for Japanese immigrant women after World War II, just as it did in 1908 with the

Gentlemen's Agreement. As in the case of Japanese picture brides in the early twentieth century, Japanese women were once again granted entry as wives only—this time as wives to American men—showing again that even in times of exclusion, exceptions were made for wives of respectable men. But in the case of Japanese immigrant women, marriage was the only means of inclusion until 1965. During the Allied Occupation of Japan, however, marriage as a means of inclusion was redefined in terms of the American servicemen and civil rights discourses. Japanese women's subordination to men under military rule would not only facilitate their immigration to the US but also their lived experiences once in America.

Furthermore, the marriage discourse that emerged around Black-Japanese marriages was shaped by Afro-Asian thinking that predated the war. Black Americans had expressed pro-Japanese solidarity as early as the turn of the twentieth century. This expression of Afro-Asian solidarity grew as Japan rose as a non-white world power in the prewar era, becoming what many viewed as the "champion of the darker races."[18] Some Japanese also expressed solidarity with Black Americans in an attempt to gain their support.[19] By the time of the Japanese defeat and the subsequent Allied Occupation, much of the Afro-Asian fervor of the prewar and war years dissipated, only to be taken up in later years during the civil rights era. However, the immediate post-World War II years did not necessarily mark a lull in Afro-Asian activity; instead, it found new expressions in the intimate encounters between African American men and Japanese women.[20] This period saw a flourishing of Black-Japanese romantic relationships resulting in a number of highly-visible marriages.[21]

The Southernization of Japan

In the summer of 1950, Katherine Davenport, an African American woman working for the US Army in Japan, wrote to her brother-in-law, Clifford R. Moore, a lawyer in Trenton, New Jersey, describing the "nastiest situation recently encountered" by Black GIs serving in the Allied Occupation of Japan. According to Davenport, the occupation forces controlled four swimming pools throughout Tokyo, all of which were open to Allied personnel. The Meiji pool was the finest of all, for it had been built for the 1940 Summer Olympic Games in Tokyo, which never took place. The Meiji pool was also the closest to the depot where Davenport was based. As the director of an army service club in Tokyo, Davenport wanted to treat the servicemen affiliated with her club to a "splash party" at the pool. However, when the men arrived, they were turned away. The US military had issued a memo declaring the pool off-limits to Black GIs. "Appalled" and "angry," Davenport wrote to her brother-in-law seeking guidance: "Can't I do something? What course of action would you suggest?" she asked.[22]

Davenport believed the racial tensions in Tokyo were the result of the US military presence in Japan. She blamed the "deep influence" of the US military's "Southern element" for reproducing Jim Crow in Tokyo. Citing the high number of white Southern men in the US Army, she lamented that "the racial discrimination here is as flagrant as it is in Georgia." The fact that the pool was the site of such "flagrant" racial discrimination should have come as no surprise to Davenport and Moore. Just a few years after Davenport penned her letter to the NAACP, the civil rights organization challenged racial segregation in Baltimore public pools.[23] Historically, public swimming pools were the site of racial tensions since they began popping up throughout urban and suburban communities in the 1920s and 30s. Swimming pools were an especially contested site of racial tension as they were seen as intimate and erotic public spaces that allowed—indeed encouraged—gender integration.[24] What was different about the Meiji incident, however, was that it occurred on Japanese soil.

In her plea to Moore, Davenport acknowledged the linkages between discrimination against Black Americans in Japan at the hands of Japanese civilians and the spreading of ideas of white supremacy: "In many places such as the P.X. [the post exchange] and commissary one can notice how the Japanese clerks in so many instances turn without question to wait on a white face first." For Davenport, the denial of swimming privileges at the fine Meiji pool and the favoring of white patrons by Japanese clerks amounted to a "slap in the face" to the men who were bravely serving the United States.[25] However, Davenport did not view the Japanese mistreatment of Black Americans in the PX exchanges as evidence of Japanese antiblackness. It was the US military influence on the Japanese that produced their antiblack attitudes and behaviors. From the perspective of Black Americans, the Japanese were mere bystanders easily influenced by the US military. Davenport's refusal to hold the Japanese accountable for their display of antiblack prejudice was perhaps influenced by a sense of Afro-Asian unity that gained traction in the Black press in the first decades of the twentieth century. Or perhaps in refusing to acknowledge Japanese civilians own antiblackness Davenport was drawing from Orientalist ideas that viewed the Japanese, and Asian people more broadly, as impotent and non-threatening.[26]

Davenport's brother-in-law, Clifford R. Moore, happened to be a World War I veteran and civil rights attorney who had recently gained prominence after he, along with Thurgood Marshall and Raymond Pace Alexander, defended the Trenton Six in an appeal following their conviction. Considered the northern counterpart to the Scottsboro Boys, the Trenton Six were a group of Black men in New Jersey wrongfully accused of murdering a white shopkeeper. Moore was integral to the overturning of the death penalty for the young men, as well as to the acquittal of four of the six men in 1951.[27] After the trial, he continued to practice law in New Jersey and was appointed US Commissioner in 1952.[28] As both a World War I veteran and civil rights attorney, Moore was qualified to advise Davenport on matters of racial discrimination in the military.

After receiving Davenport's letter, Moore wrote to Roy Wilkins of the NAACP relating Davenport's concern. In return, Roy Wilkins wrote to Frank Pace Jr., the Army Secretary, detailing the claims laid bare by Davenport and Moore and demanding an "immediate investigation of the matter."[29] Moore's own experience in the military also heightened his concern for Black GIs in Japan. In his letter to Wilkins, Moore referenced General Edward M. Almond, the white commanding officer of the all-Black Ninety-Second Division, the only all-Black unit to see combat during World War I. Almond faced allegations of racial misconduct in his training and commandment of the division, and had since become a symbol of racial prejudice in the US military. Moore wrote, "I can readily understand the present situation as it exists, at least in the Tokyo area, if Gen. Almond has anything to do with the command or policy of the Tokyo command." Despite Moore and Davenport's efforts, the Secretary of the Army did not take action. In his response to the NAACP, Pace dismissed allegations of racial discrimination, citing Executive Order 9981 issued in 1948 by President Truman, which abolished racial discrimination and segregation in the armed forces. For Pace, the allegations of racial discrimination were mere "generalities" and not indicative of systemic, racial discrimination in the military.[30]

However, racial discrimination in the military did exist. African American troops often occupied the lowest ranks within the military, held the lowest-paid jobs, and were the frequent target of white military violence. In 1946—four years before Davenport penned her letter to Moore—the 1940th Engineer Aviation Utilities Company (EAUC) stationed outside Tokyo wrote an open letter describing the racial violence inflicted on African American members of the company. The servicemen described a number of violent incidents where white GIs from a neighboring station had beaten, stabbed, and mutilated Black GIs. These acts of violence, according to the men of 1940th EAUC, showed the Japanese people the true nature of American democracy: one steeped in racial prejudice. The letter ends with the exclamation: "Mr. Bilbo's wildest dream for America has come true here in Japan. We suggest that he move to the Far East, where his paradise has already been made."[31] The servicemen of 1940th EAUC were referring to Theodore G. Bilbo, a Mississippi senator and well-known white supremacist. Senator Bilbo sought to block racial progress at every turn, and became a symbol of white southern bigotry. In 1947 Bilbo published *Take Your Choice: Separation or Mongrelization*, in which he argued for the deportation of African Americans to Africa in an effort to preserve racial purity of the races.[32] By ending their open letter with a reference to Bilbo, the men of 1940th EAUC showed that they understood racial violence in Japan to be an extension of the racial attitudes that ruled the American South.[33]

The African American press also took note of the unequal treatment of Black GIs in the European Theater of Operations (ETO), where a pattern of racial discrimination took root in court martial cases involving Black GIs accused of rape. In France, many African American GIs were scapegoated as rapists out of fear and anxiety about war, defeat, and the growing power of the US following World War II. The Black press was key in publicizing how Black servicemen in France were disproportionately accused of rape and subsequently denied due process trials.[34] The unequal treatment of Black GIs in France was also viewed as an American export from the South, just as it was in Japan.[35]

Afro-Asian Solidarity

In 1936, fourteen years before Davenport penned her letter to Moore, W.E.B. Du Bois visited Japan as an invited guest of two leading Japanese daily newspapers. Du Bois painted a flattering picture of the Japanese and their perceived sympathy towards the plight of African Americans in a series of recollections published by the *Pittsburgh Courier*.[36] Du Bois expressed in detail just how well he was treated in Japan, and he often positioned his positive experiences with the Japanese people in sharp contrast to his hostile experiences with white Americans. In 1937, he wrote:

> On the last day, as I was paying my bill at the Imperial Hotel of Tokyo, a typical loud-mouthed American white women barged in and demanded service. In America the clerk would have immediately turned to her, if not to wait on her[,] at least to apologize or explain. But not in Tokyo. The Clerk did not wink an eye or turn his head; he carefully finished waiting on me and took time to bow with Japanese politeness and then turned to America.[37]

Du Bois reported that his warm welcome in Japan was not meant for him alone, but for all Black Americans suffering under Jim Crow. Du Bois's treatment in Japan, according to Du Bois himself, was meant as recognition of a common bond between the Japanese and Black Americans. This bond was made under the common suffering both groups experienced under white supremacy, and strengthened in a common desire to resist western rule.[38]

As early as 1905, when the Japanese defeated Russia in the Russo-Japanese War, Du Bois made public declarations of his pro-Japanese stance by pointing to the interconnectedness of the Black freedom struggle in the US and Japan's struggle to abate western encroachment and establish itself as a powerful Asian country free from western dominance. Du Bois's pro-Japanese writings were part of larger movement among Black Americans across the US in the first decades of the twentieth century that sympathized with the Japanese struggle for autonomy.[39] Pro-Japanese sentiment was expressed in the practices and rhetoric of Black nationalist groups like the Nation of Islam and Marcus Garvey's

Universal Negro Improvement Association, as well as in works of fiction and the Black press. Black leaders like Booker T. Washington as well as ordinary Black folk expressed admiration for Japan and Asian people more broadly.[40] As World War II wore on and Americans learned of Japanese aggression against other Asian people, Black Americans continued to support Japan. Some, including Du Bois, went so far as to justify the atrocities committed by the Japanese.[41] This pro-Japanese stance translated into romantic visions of Afro-Asian solidarity for Black men serving in the Allied Occupation. This does not mean that racial tensions between African Americans and the Japanese did not exist; surely they did. However, a belief in a Black-Japanese alliance dating back to the early twentieth century shaped much of the Black experience in Occupied Japan. Black GIs in Japan saw clear affinities between themselves and the Japanese.[42]

Interracial Intimacies in Occupied Japan

In January 1947, the all-Black Twenty-Fourth Infantry Regiment landed at the port of Kobe, and soon after, arrived at Camp Gifu, located at the center of the main island. Camp Gifu would become home to the Twenty-Fourth Regiment for the remainder of the Allied Occupation and during the Korean War. When the men arrived, the locals greeted them with curiosity. Fred Thomas, an enlisted soldier with the Twenty-Fourth Regiment, recalled that upon seeing the soldiers for the first time, Japanese children licked their fingers then rubbed the soldier's skin to see if their skin color would rub off. Recounting these interactions, Thomas explained, "they called us *chocoleta* soldiers" and asked, "why you no *washa washa*?"[43] Charles L. Glittens of Cambridge, Massachusetts, recalled a similar scenario during his stay in Yokohama in 1946: "The Japanese people loved us. We were called the chocolate soldiers. I didn't run into any Black soldier who objected to that because that was the Japanese way of saying, 'We love you, chocolate soldiers!'"[44] Despite these awkward initial encounters which may have otherwise signaled antiblack animus among the Japanese, real tensions between the Japanese locals and the Twenty-Fourth Regiment at Camp Gifu were rare, according to Thomas.[45] African American servicemen and their families stationed in Japan reportedly made themselves quite at home at Camp Gifu.[46]

After a tour of duty throughout Japan, Corporal John Paul of Mount Vernon, New York, explained that the Japanese people were "genuine friends of colored people." He recalled, "There is not prejudice against our race among the Japanese. They seem to feel allied to us as people of color and have a deep respect for the colored soldier and value his friendship highly."[47] Sidney Jordan, who arrived in Yokohama in 1949, explained: "Most of the white guys, they were so super critical, you can always hear them abusing the Japanese, calling them gooks and things like that. But the Black guys, they didn't do that. So [the Japanese] had a better affinity with the Black fellows. We didn't have any problem."[48] Rather, the source of much of the racial tension that did exist came from white military personnel and the military more broadly.[49]

Though the Japanese had been in contact with Americans before the war, this new era saw significant interaction between Japanese women and African American servicemen in particular. During the occupation of Japan, thousands of American men and Japanese women formed intimate relationships, resulting in a large number of marriages. Between 1947 and 1953, 7,153 Japanese women immigrated to the United States as wives of American citizens.[50] When Cpl. Paul spoke of the Japanese tendency to value African American friendship, he was speaking from personal experience. In 1948, Paul married Heidako Nakamura, a "fetching, dark-eyed night club singer."[51] As a child, Paul starred in the Broadway musical *Hellzapoppin* and went on to become a French horn player and tour Japan with the 289th Army Band Unit. Paul's account of friendly relations between African Americans and the Japanese belies the tension that existed in the PX exchanges and swimming pools that Davenport described, but it also points to a different kind of encounter during this historical moment. For Paul, the racial discrimination that Black GIs experienced both on and off the base was softened by the "vital creolized counterculture" of the occupation where music and dancing played an important role in facilitating social relations.[52] It is within this flourishing subculture that Paul met Nakamura.

Sumiko and Willie Brown met while jitterbugging outside an American USO club in Tokyo that Willie helped to manage. Sumiko and her friends had become enthusiastic jitterbuggers before the war. After the war, Sumiko explained, the only place you could hear jazz was at the American servicemen's clubs. In the still-segregated US military, African

American clubs were the only ones to play jazz. Too shy to go in, Sumiko and her friends danced together underneath an open window. Willie, the club's assistant manager, spotted the women and invited them in.[53] Similarly, in 1948 Sgt. First Class Emanuel Lewis met Etsuko Yonamoto at the opening of a Black servicemen's club in Yokohama on Lewis's thirty-second birthday. The two danced and dated for two years before marrying in 1950.[54] Despite the antiblack prejudices in Occupied Japan, a thriving subculture fueled by music and drink emerged. Takamae Eiji explains that within the subculture of Occupied Japan, "many of Japan's leading postwar jazz artists and popular entertainers got their start . . . undisturbed by convention and the prying eyes of whites." Relationships between Japanese women and Black GIs flourished within this postwar counterculture.[55]

According to Cpl. Paul, Japanese women preferred dating Black GIs over whites. The Japanese, he declared, had much to teach white American soldiers about "the futility of white supremacy."[56] Cpl. Paul's report echoed earlier declarations of Afro-Asian unity by prominent intellectuals like Du Bois. However, Paul's idealized description of Black-Japanese interactions was undermined by the Black press who, in reporting on unions between American men and Japanese women, perpetuated negative stereotypes of Japanese women as docile yet sexually promiscuous. Owing much to the Madame Butterfly trope, the racialized and sexualized representation of Japanese women in both the mainstream and Black press reaffirmed the unequal power dynamics between the conquerors and the conquered. These discrepancies reveal a complicated system of power that privileged American heterosexual men—both Black and white—over the Japanese. Though Black GIs had to contend with racial hostility and violence, low-ranking jobs, and unequal pay, when it came to the Japanese, they were still members of the conquering nation. Simply put, despite their circumscribed positions within the United States military, as American victors of war they had access to heterosexual male privilege.[57]

The relationships between Black American men and Japanese women occurred at a time when articulations about the nature of a Japan-US Cold War alliance were being played out in the press and elsewhere. After World War II, Americans became interested in East Asia in unprecedented ways. This changing dynamic was influenced by the expansion of US power in Asia as part of the anticommunism efforts of the Truman administration. But before Americans could fully embrace US foreign policy abroad, they had to first be persuaded to do the same at home. American influencers—writers, journalists, filmmakers, educators, and government officials—propagandized the threat of communist Asia to gain support for US containment policies. Japanese war brides married to American GIs were part of a controlled narrative that helped secure widespread support for the Cold War alliance between Japan and the US.[58] In a strategic geopolitical move, these "Cold War Intellectuals" championed the United States as a beacon of racial tolerance and big brother to the downtrodden and defeated Japanese Empire. This narrative were popularized as the United States anticipated conflicts with the communist superpowers in North Korea and the Soviet Union. A timely alliance between the US and Japan was therefore forged in the US press, and Japanese war brides came to represent the possibilities of a postwar Japan-US union.

However, the shift in American attitudes towards the Japanese came at a high cost. In postwar public discourse, Japanese women were portrayed as hypersexualized victims of Japanese patriarchy, which perpetuated the harmful stereotypes that justified the US occupation of Japan.[59] To add insult to injury, the Black press drew on the image of Black-Japanese unions to undermine Black womanhood. Japanese women were celebrated as model wives to Black men for they were perceived as subservient and eager to please.[60]

For their part, Japanese women seemed largely motivated to marry American men to escape the yoke of Japanese tradition. Many of the women possessed an adventurous spirit, but they were also enticed by the "American way of life" represented by the consumer goods American GIs had at their disposal.[61] Chizuko Murata met Clifford Watkins, a Black American GI stationed in Yokohama, in 1949. Described as a generous and caring man, Clifford courted Chizuko, often bringing small gifts like chocolate and bottles of Coca-Cola to her and her family. Two years later the two were married, and in 1952 they moved to the US.[62] Women like Chizuko were the predecessors of the generation of Japanese women who would later stake their claim in a foreign land in an attempt to "defect" from their expected life courses in Japan. For Japanese women, intimacy with American men meant opportunity. Women like Chizuko engaged in a form of "sexualized agency" that resulted in what anthropologist Karen Kelsky describes as the "potent conflation of fantasy and opportunity."[63] In war-torn Japan, American men had candy, soda, and jazz; and they were generous. They could also dance. They arrived strong and healthy and eager to make friends with the Japanese. They were utterly irresistible, according to some Japanese women even more than fifty years later.[64]

Meanwhile, entire generations of young Japanese men had either perished in the war, were imprisoned in war camps along the Pacific awaiting repatriation, or were working menial jobs under the command of the Allied forces. Crockett observed a frustrated Japanese man lamenting the unequal treatment of Japanese men and women by the Allied forces. "Why is it . . . that Americans blame us—the men—for everything yet seem to think our women are wonderful?" he asked. To him, Japanese men were living ghosts of a recent past that many wished to forget. In response, Crockett suggested, "Japanese men and women might be two different races entirely."[65]

Despite this new era of contact, interracial relationships between Japanese women and non-Japanese men was not unprecedented. In the early modern era, the Japanese intermarried with Koreans and Chinese. In the late sixteenth century after the Portuguese established a trade relationship at Nagasaki, many Japanese women who had converted to Catholicism married Portuguese men and left the country.[66] In 1600, Japanese women began to marry Dutch and Englishmen. These relationships were encouraged and celebrated by Japanese society.[67] But in 1636 under the threat of encroaching foreigners and their religious influence, officials instituted anti-Christian policies and a ban on interracial marriage. The ban was not created out of concerns about race-mixing but rather a concern for protecting Japanese sovereignty from foreign religion. Yet even during the age of seclusion, Japanese women and foreign men continued to have intimate contact. After Commodore Perry's arrival in 1852, relationships between Japanese and non-Japanese once again flourished. Though interracial marriages were not novel to Japanese culture, the intimate contact between Black American men and Japanese women was still unprecedented.

To be sure, intimate relationships may not have only occurred between American men and Japanese women; it is a strong possibility that American women and Japanese men had relationships in Occupied Japan as well. In France, African American soldiers were hostile to Black servicewomen who socialized with and dated white French civilians.[68] In Japan, Black American women had consistent contact with Japanese men who worked in the service industry.

African American women's experience differed from their male counterparts. In her plea to Moore, Davenport acknowledged that she had never experienced racial discrimination by the Japanese. Sylvia J. Rock, an American Red Cross worker in Japan from 1950–51, commented that her "first impression of Tokyo was a pleasant revelation." Rock was surprised to find that, not only did Tokyo feel like a large American city with skyscrapers, automobiles, and organized traffic patterns, but she also found herself in "possession of a maid" as well. Though she enjoyed the services bequeathed to her, it also embarrassed her since she felt "perfectly capable of washing her clothes and keeping her room tidy."[69] Rock also noted her surprise that educated Japanese men were performing the "lowest tasks" for low wages. In addition to service industry labor, Japanese soldiers were returning home to work as stevedores on docks, replacing "Tan Yanks as laborers" under the watchful eye of the American military, according to the *Baltimore Afro American* in 1945.[70] Despite being relegated to perform menial labor, Rock noted that Japanese men never lost their sense of humor or dignity.[71]

Like their male counterparts, Black women in the armed forces stood in a unique place of privilege with respect to the Japanese people.[72] In Occupied Japan, the US military offered decent salaries and benefits that went further than they would have in the US. Ethel Payne, a journalist and the director of the American Red Cross service club in Tokyo, spent most of her time away from work traveling throughout Japan. As an African American woman in Occupied Japan, Payne had access to goods and services that may have been out of reach to her in the United States. Payne and others like her reported enjoying such activities as shopping and socializing on their time off. Indeed, in Japan, both Black and white Americans hired servants, shopped, and traveled throughout the country with relative ease.[73]

While African American women exercised a certain level of purchasing power in Japan, it did not negate the racial discrimination of the military. In the summer of 1949, Lt. Millie Susan Hooks of the Army Nurse Corps was abruptly dismissed from service. Hooks suspected that her dismissal was the result of poor relations between herself and her direct superior—presumably a white man—and not her poor performance, as he had claimed. Once stateside, Hooks sought the legal aid of the NAACP. The NAACP charged the military with discrimination on Hooks's behalf, as well as on behalf of another Black army nurse who had filed a complaint before Hooks. In their filing, the NAACP pointed to the racial segregation of the army hospital where Hooks and the other woman were employed. Ultimately, the case went nowhere as the military denied the NAACP access to records pertaining to Hooks and her dismissal. These various, contradicting experiences of Black women members of the occupation personnel show how race and gender intersected in different but powerful ways.[74] It also reveals the influence that unprecedented access to commercial goods and services in Occupied Japan had on Black Americans' favorable perceptions of the Japanese. In this way, Du Bois's experience in Japan in the 1930s was similar to Black Americans experience in Occupied Japan. Racial tensions between African Americans and the Japanese undoubtedly existed, but such tensions were often overlooked demonstrating how deeply-ingrained the pro-Japanese sentiment was among Black Americans. Importantly, the overwhelmingly positive narratives that African Americans shared about race relations in Japan suggests just how deeply the American racial order impacted their experiences abroad.

Interracial Marriage and Civil Rights

Black GIs wishing to marry Japanese women faced fierce resistance from the military. Black servicemen publicly and privately opposed such restrictions, demanding the equal right to marry and father children. In their struggle for marital equality, African American servicemen in the Pacific looked to the NAACP for aid. Their actions marked a shift in the role that interracial marriage would play in civil rights discourse throughout the midcentury. In November 1949, George Brown, an Army corporal serving with the occupation forces in Japan, wrote the legal committee of the NAACP pleading for help. According to Brown, he and other men in his company had met and fell in love with Japanese women whom they now wished to marry and bring to the United States, but the US military stood in their way. In his letter, Brown addressed racial discrimination against Japanese women by the US military. He recognized that his compatriots serving in Europe were allowed to marry and bring their European brides home to the States, arguing that the restrictions imposed against Japanese brides were indicative of the pervasiveness of anti-Asian sentiment in the military and US immigration policy. He wrote:

> Surely I am as much in love with my girl and baby as anyone else. [If] legislative laws permit the GIs with German and other European wives and children to marry and enter our country, why should a line be drawn against people of the East? . . . If the babies of GIs born to European mothers are thought of by the Army, why can't the babies born to Japanese mothers be thought of too? Aren't they all part American? Doesn't our democracy advocate that all peoples, regardless of race creed or color, are equal?[75]

Brown understood that the policies that restricted American men from marrying Japanese women were a reflection of Jim Crow discrimination that now extended to the Japanese. Brown's letter also reveals the hypocrisy of American democracy. At the same time that the US claimed to be a beacon of tolerance in light of the racial and religious atrocities of the war, the nation's racial minorities endured acts of racial discrimination and violence both at home and abroad. Implicit in Brown's plea was the notion that US military service should beget basic civil rights, including the freedom to marry whom one chooses.[76]

Brown's emphasis on his unconditional love for his Japanese girlfriend and their child may have been in response to criticism of American-Japanese relationships, particularly between Black men and Japanese women, from military personnel such as Elizabeth Ryan, an American civilian employee in Occupied Japan. In her letters home, Ryan, a provost court reporter for the Inspector General in Kobe, Japan from 1947 to 1948, often wrote about the marriages between American servicemen and Japanese women. In August 1947, Ryan wrote a letter discrediting

African American soldiers who married Japanese women. She claimed that after the War Bride Act of 1947 was passed, American GIs in Japan rushed to marry Japanese women to collect additional rations for their wives, implying that necessity, perhaps even materialistic desire, and not "true" love, compelled the soldiers to marry. Furthermore, she claimed that Black GIs hastily married Japanese women for sex only.[77] Ryan's words echoed criticism from Americans—both Black and white—in Occupied Japan who disapproved of the unions between Black GIs and Japanese women. When Corporal Brown wrote to the NAACP in 1949, four years into the occupation, he was surely aware of the white military personnel who vehemently disapproved of Black-Japanese interracial marriages.

Brown's letter made quite an impact, for just days later on December 1, 1949, Jack Greenberg, Assistant Special Counsel for the NAACP Legal Defense and Educational Fund, wrote to the Secretary of Defense "concerning the problem of the marriage of American soldiers to Japanese women."[78] Greenberg asked James C. Evans, Civilian Assistant to the Secretary of Defense, for assistance in aiding African American servicemen who wished to marry Japanese women in Occupied Japan, citing Corporal Brown's letter. A few weeks later Evans wrote back to Greenberg mirroring Frank Pace's response to Moore and Davenport's accusations of racial discrimination at the Meiji pool: "[An] investigation revealed that there is no current prohibition regarding the marriage of American soldiers to Japanese nationals, although the granting of permission for such marriage is left to the discretion of the Overseas Commanders."[79] Evans's response shows how the military refused to be a laboratory for social change.[80] Denying that racial discrimination existed in marriage policy and leaving the final decision to commanders meant that the military could absolve itself from accusations of racial discrimination, while at the local level, commanders could continue to deny permission to marry. Such barriers led many Black soldiers and Japanese women to marry in Shinto ceremonies, a traditional Japanese wedding consisting of ancient and modern elements. Such marriages were not legal in the eyes of the US military or Immigration Service.[81] In these instances, husband and wife would eventually have to marry again, this time with the permission of the US military.

James Evans's letter to Jack Greenberg touched on another crucial obstacle faced by couples when he wrote, "Japanese spouses of American servicemen may encounter difficulty in gaining entrance to the United States due to the current immigration restrictions and quotas, and they are advised of this obstacle."[82] Because Japanese immigration to the United States had been restricted since the passage of the National Origin Act in 1924, Evans could cite immigration law—an area out of his jurisdiction—to deny American GIs and Japanese women the right to marry. In the end, Evans's dismissive letter did nothing to "alleviate the plight" of the soldiers. Greenberg wrote to Brown on December 28, 1949: "I regret that there is nothing further that we can do, but please be assured that you have our best wishes."[83] It is unclear whether Corporal George Brown was able to eventually marry his Japanese girlfriend. One can only hope that he eventually succeeded, as many of his fellow compatriots did, after a series of acts were enacted that specifically allowed Japanese women to enter the United States as brides to servicemen.[84]

In addition to these legal barriers, Black servicemen and Japanese women faced targeted acts of sabotage committed by the United States military personnel. In 1952, *The Chicago Defender* reported that nearly 400 African American servicemen from the all-Black Twenty-Fourth Infantry Regiment stationed at Camp Gifu were being subjected to discriminatory military practices that prevented them from marrying their Japanese girlfriends. War correspondent L. Alex Wilson explained that "some high officials have indicated that steps may be taken to keep the regiment from returning to camp, thus keeping marriage vows unspoken." According to Wilson, many of the men were now "engaged in mopping up activity in North Korea" and were waiting to return to Japan to marry their Japanese sweethearts. However, if the military had its way, the men would be reassigned, or sent back to the States in a deliberate attempt to sabotage their relationships with Japanese women. Wilson also explained how many of the men had fathered children before being deployed to North Korea, and were anxiously awaiting return to Japan to be with their families.[85] The military deliberately sent African American troops to Korea in a malicious act to separate them from their Japanese sweethearts.

In "Why Tan Yanks Go for Japanese Girls" published in the *Chicago Defender*, Wilson explained that if the soldiers of the Twenty-Fourth

Regiment were sent to North Korea, then demobilized or reassigned to prevent them from returning to Camp Gifu, a profusion of fatherless Black-Japanese babies would be left behind in Japan. The result would be a repetition of the "brown baby" situation that occurred in Europe during World War II, when African American soldiers engaged in intimate relationships with European women, leaving behind hundreds of illegitimate, mixed-race babies when they returned home to the United States.[86] The possibility of such an outcome in Japan undoubtedly loomed large in the minds of men like George Brown. After their removal from Japan, many Black GIs never again saw their Japanese sweethearts nor their half-Japanese children again.[87]

African American GIs stationed in the European Theater of Operations (ETO) also encountered restrictive marriage policies. Black servicemen in Europe were prevented from marrying their European girlfriends on the grounds that marriage between a white woman and Black man was illegal in nearly half of the fifty states. Unlike Japan, restriction in Europe was wholly based on antiblack sentiments in the military. German, French, English and Italian brides who married white American GIs had far more ease in marrying and immigrating to the US than their Japanese counterparts.[88] In a 1946 letter to the NAACP, Robert Bradford, an African American soldier serving in the ETO, addressed his frustration at not being permitted to marry and bring home his European girlfriend. Bradford explained that Black servicemen were being denied permission to marry foreign girlfriends who were in many cases the mothers of their children: "There are many soldiers who would love to make their child and its mother happy, but this American prejudice doesn't allow it."[89] Similarly, in his letter to the NAACP, Brown wrote: "In my outfit alone which consists of less than a hundred men, there are eight soldiers that have children born of Japanese mothers, and each and everyone of them are praying for our country to lift the barrier that is keeping them from being united with their children."[90] By denying men like Bradford and Brown the right to marry, the military was preventing them from entering into a state-sanctioned relationship. The rights and privileges extended to married couples—especially those who were members of the armed forces—lay beyond their reach. However, both men were facing different legislative barriers. Bradford was denied permission to marry because the union between an African American man and a white

European woman would violate anti-miscegenation laws in the United States. Brown was denied permission to marry because Japanese citizens remained barred from entering the United States.

It was not only the "lovesick" soldiers who understood the racial discrimination embedded in military regulations.[91] In December of 1945, Walter White, head of the NAACP, wrote to the Secretary of War on behalf of soldiers like Bradford and Brown asking that the military take immediate steps to correct the prejudice. White stated that the NAACP had received several requests for assistance from Black soldiers abroad wishing to marry their foreign sweethearts. White accused the US military of acting as "partners to bastardry."[92] By preventing African American GIs from marrying their foreign girlfriends and establishing a legitimate, respectable family unit, the United States military was perpetuating what W.E.B. Du Bois called the "red-stain of bastardry," which disproportionally affected the children of African American descent.[93]

Conclusion

The NAACP's involvement in Black GI marriages marked a shift in the organization's approach towards marriage equality. In the first half of the twentieth century, the NAACP had been reluctant to challenge miscegenation laws in court. When the association did, it argued for the "natural" or "fundamental" right to marry.[94] According to Peter Wallenstein, the NAACP "was slow . . . to take an aggressive stance toward miscegenation laws already in place. It was a question of priorities. . . . Desegregation on the marriage front seemed far less pressing a matter than did progress in educational opportunity or voting rights."[95] But in 1962, the organization began to challenge anti-miscegenation laws based on arguments for civil rights and racial integration. The protests of Black GIs both in the European Theater of Operations and the Pacific led to the organization's shift, putting them at the forefront of marriage equality and civil rights activism. This new articulation of what constituted a civil right was made concrete by the service and sacrifices the GIs made in defending American democracy during the war. Again, as in the early twentieth century, marriage was key to Japanese women's immigration, as well as to the full citizenship of the Black men they married.

For the Japanese women involved, the issues of marriage and immigration were part of a longer history of Japanese women's immigration to the United States. Like the Gentlemen's Agreement of 1908, the War Bride Acts were devised to allow Japanese women to enter the United States. What was different this time around was that the women came as wives to American servicemen of all racial backgrounds—many Japanese American GIs (Nisei) did in fact marry and bring home Japanese brides. Their arrival in the US was made legitimate by the military service of their husbands. For Japanese women, then, immigration to the United States was contingent upon their role within a heteropatriarchal relationship. For Japanese immigrant women in the US, marriage proved the "price of admission."[96]

Furthermore, the intimate relationships between Black men and Japanese women were shaped by a perceived affinity between the Japanese and African Americans that dated back to the early twentieth century. Though at times these encounters were transactional, they were also embedded in a larger genealogy of Afro-Asian thinking, at least from the perspective of Black men in Japan. In this way, racial solidarity between Black Americans and the Japanese could be said to have materialized in intimate ways during the Allied Occupation of Japan. These relationships contributed to new ways of thinking about the connections between interracial intimacy and civil rights in the post-World War II era.

4

"A Bridge Between East and West"

Domesticity and Citizenship in the Making of Japanese War Brides

Bear in mind always: "Because of my husband and his love for me, I am going to be a loyal American. I will do my part to help in that country any way I can. It is my country now and my children's."
—Camp Kokura Brides School, American Red Cross, Japan 1956

In 1949, Thomas Radtke, an army medical corpsman stationed in Kobe, Japan met a nurse named Mitsuko Ito. Radtke, a native of Chicago, Illinois, born and raised in a devout Catholic home, wrote to his parents explaining that he and Mitsuko had "fallen in love" and wished to marry in Chicago. Thomas was Andrew and Loretta Radtke's only child and the two were "very much in favor" of their son's engagement because, as they explained, Mitsuko was "studying to be a Catholic and our son had fallen away from the church, now she has him returning to the church for which we are ever grateful."[1] However, the National Origins Act of 1924 prohibited Mitsuko from entering the United States. When Congress passed the GI Brides Act of 1945 to "ease" the entry of brides of American servicemen, Asian women were excluded. The act favored the European brides of American men. Then, in 1947 the Alien Brides Act was passed permitting Japanese women otherwise deemed "racially ineligible" to enter the United States as wives. However, the 1947 act mandated that the couples had to marry and apply for citizenship within a thirty-day time frame following the act's passage. But Thomas Radtke and Mitsuko Ito did not meet until 1949, and the special legislation permitting Japanese women to enter the US as brides was of no use to them. Soon after hearing of their son's dilemma, the Radtkes reached out to Richard Akagi, the director of the Japanese American Citizens

League's Midwest office. Akagi suggested they write to their congressional representative, Sidney R. Yates, to ask if special legislation could be introduced on Mitsuko's behalf. In June 1950, with the aid of Congressman Yates, Private Law 614 was passed allowing Mitsuko entry into the US as Radtke's fiancé.

However, the terms were conditional. Upon her arrival to the US, Ito was given three months to marry Radtke and apply for permanent residency to prove her "bona fide intention" to marry an American citizen; otherwise, she would face deportation under the Immigration Act of 1917.[2] As a Japanese woman, Ito was inadmissible because of race, but as the wife of an American serviceman, she was permitted entry and a pathway to citizenship. Therefore, marriage determined Ito's immigration status and legitimized her presence in the US, ultimately binding her relationship with Radtke to her legal status and social identity in the United States.

Despite these efforts, Radtke was unable to return to the US with Ito to marry. Soon after the passage of Private Law 614, North Korean forces crossed the 38th parallel into South Korea, ushering in the start of the Korean War. Concerned, Radtke wrote to Congressman Yates asking if, in the event he was shipped to Korea, Ito could be sent to the US to be with his parents; for he reasoned, "they might be able to comfort each other" in his absence. Yates informed Radtke that he would have to obtain permission from Occupation authorities, but offered to "cut some of the red tape" by writing to the Adjutant General of the Army on Thomas and Mitsuko's behalf.[3] But there was no need to worry, Radtke made it back from Korea unharmed and after much bureaucratic wrangling, he married Ito in Japan the following year and eventually returned to the United States to settle. Thomas Radtke and Mitsuko Ito's story was hardly unusual. In the years after WWII, many young American servicemen navigated restrictive immigration laws and bureaucratic barriers—in many cases with the assistance of family members and local government representatives—to gain permission to marry and bring home their Japanese fiancés and brides. Between 1950 and 1952, in his congressional district alone, which covered a section of the north side of Chicago, Congressmen Yates assisted fifteen American servicemen, many of them Nisei.

The first recorded Japanese war bride entered the United States in 1947, just two years after the defeat of the Japanese Empire. Between 1947 and 1955, nearly 13,000 Japanese women immigrated to the United States as wives of American military personnel.[4] They arrived as wives to American men of all racial and ethnic backgrounds. One in every four unions was between a Japanese woman and a Nisei or African American GI.[5] Marriage was central to Japanese women's immigration after World War II, just as it had been in the era of the Gentlemen's Agreement, but so too was the military service of the men they married. The expansion of immigration policy to include war brides received bipartisan support that "stressed the debt owed to military personnel."[6] Even the American Legion, known for its nativist agenda, issued a resolution at its national convention in October 1948 in support of legislation allowing the naturalization of parents or the spouse of veterans of the armed forces regardless of race or national origin.[7]

Between 1924 and 1952, immigration laws barred Japanese nationals from immigrating to the US—for they were deemed racially inferior and unable to assimilate. Yet as Martha Gardner has shown, even in times of exclusion, wives maintained a privileged position in immigration policy.[8] While immigration restrictions barred the Japanese—and all Asian immigrants—from entering the country, the Alien Bride Act made an exception for the wives of US military personnel. To be sure, the act was not intended to empower immigrant women, but extend the rights and privileges of their military-citizen husbands.

The series of bride acts in the immediate postwar period occurred in an era that heroicized the American GI. During the war the US encouraged civilian worship of the combat soldier to gain both symbolic and material support for the war. Afterwards, the wartime hero worship of the combat soldier led to GI entitlements, which included the GI Bill.[9] The freedom to marry non-American women was an integral part of the postwar privileges bestowed to American GIs for their service. As Senator Richard Russel, Jr (D-Ga.) argued in 1945, it was "the least we can do for the men who fought our wars overseas."[10] Similar to the Gentlemen's Agreement in 1908, the Alien Bride Act explicitly reinforced the patriarchal standards of US immigration control by allowing Japanese women to enter only as brides.[11] Their entrance into the United States was contingent on their status as wives and mothers.[12] This time, however, they entered as brides to American servicemen.

As military wives, these women became part of a powerful institution that relied upon a "masculine ethos" to achieve its political imperatives. As Cynthia Enloe has described, the military valued "wifely femininity" to the extent that it could bolster "militarized masculinity."[13] In other words, wives reinforced the masculine power of husbands to the benefit of the US military. The presence of Japanese women was made possible and legitimated by two institutions—the United States military and marriage—both of which relied on the domestic capabilities of women to maintain and extend American masculine power. In return, military wives gained access to certain privileges. For Japanese women married to American servicemen between 1945 and 1952, when the vast majority of Japanese nationals were barred from entering the United States, these privileges included the opportunity to immigrate to the US and gain a pathway to citizenship.[14] In addition, during the occupation, Japanese citizens were barred from traveling outside of Japan. Only those who married foreign citizens were allowed to leave the country. Marriage, thus, accorded mobility. But before Japanese women could enter the US, they first had to be taught how to be an American housewife because "domesticity was the price of admission."[15]

Teaching Domesticity and Citizenship

In 1948, the Christian Women's Association (CWA) in Tokyo organized the first course for Japanese brides. Another course was organized at the request of the American consulate in 1951.[16] Later that same year, the CWA and the Young Women's Christian Association (YWCA) of Tokyo came together to host another course. The following year, the American Red Cross in Tokyo became involved and eventually assumed responsibility at the request of the State Department after receiving complaints from American GIs that their Japanese wives did not make good American housewives.[17] Soon after the Red Cross takeover, a second school in Yokohama was established. The American Red Cross bride schools were designed to prepare Japanese women for successful entry into the United States by acquainting them "with the important essentials of basic, every-day living in America."[18] Over the course of several months, the women were taught English, American government and history, homemaking, child rearing, and "charm." The classes were taught lecture-style in English and translated by an interpreter. In addition to classroom instruction, home visits were arranged, allowing small groups of women to visit the American-style homes of military personnel. During home visits the bride-students were introduced to American appliances, taught to make a western bed, and were treated to a demonstration of American hospitality.

The schools were crucial sites of domestication and incorporation where Japanese women were taught the "American way of life" as their entry to the US relied on their successful training. Bride schools measured Japanese women's ability to be good wives and mothers because their immigration to the US and legal status depended upon their role within the home as well as their reproductive value in the family. In the postwar period, the importance of respectable womanhood was crucial in the ideological war between the US and Soviet Union, leading to a reaffirmation of prewar standards of domesticity and distinct gender roles for American men and women.[19] This reaffirmation of domesticity was further intensified for immigrant women because their entrance into the United States relied upon their role as wives and mothers. As the immediate post-WWII period gave way to the Cold War era, the reproductive and domestic labor of women became a source of deep concern, and Japanese immigrant women's potential contribution to the nuclear American family and the state writ large became increasingly valuable. The appearance of respectability was instrumental for Asian women's eligibility in the United States dating back to the late nineteenth and early twentieth centuries.[20]

The Red Cross bride schools began as a small enterprise run by a few volunteers and soon developed into a large-scale effort to groom Japanese women into American wives and mothers in an effort to strengthen "the link between Japan and the United States for generations to come."[21] The schools functioned as standalone courses that were offered continuously throughout the year. By 1956 the bride courses had developed a robust curriculum that combined lessons on history and geography with childcare and homemaking. The schools varied in scope and size depending on the location. The schools in Tokyo and Yokohama were the largest, as both sites were port cities with a strong US military presence from which organizers drew resources, and these schools were able to accommodate more brides than others in Japan. Tokyo graduated almost 4,000 brides between 1951 and 1957.[22]

The bride schools were organized and managed by a cadre of American women who believed it was their duty to prepare Japanese women for entry into the United States. They were the wives of American military personnel as well as single women who staked their professional aspirations in service work abroad. As these American women asserted their autonomy outside the domestic sphere—the private home as well as the nation—by seeking professional fulfillment in Japan, they simultaneously encouraged Japanese women to conform to the very roles of mother and wife that they avoided in their own lives.[23] Simply put, marriage hindered mobility for the mostly-white American women working for the Allied forces abroad, but for Japanese women who married American men, marriage was a means of achieving mobility. This difference in life choices and outcomes is a reflection of the "pan-Pacific mobility" of white women, which has historically contrasted Asian women's lack of mobility in similar contexts.[24]

The relationship between American women as teachers and Japanese women as pupils reflected the unequal relationship between Japan and the United States.[25] The US Occupation authorities, both men and women, promoted an image of ideal womanhood modeled after the supposedly progressive and democratic image of American women, while simultaneously portraying Japanese women as victims of Japanese patriarchy and imperialism. The two contrasting views were deployed to promote American democracy abroad.[26] Citing Amy Kaplan's groundbreaking analysis on the linkages between the politics of domesticity and American imperialism, Michiko Takeuchi explains: "Imposing American domesticity ideology on the Japanese was an important means of subjugating a former enemy," even when such ideologies were personally scoffed at by those promoting them. The imposition of American domesticity ideology was also "used earlier to justify subjugation of Native American and Mexicans after violent confrontations."[27] The American Red Cross bride schools were, thus, part of a longer history of the

US deploying seemingly benevolent acts of kindness within the domestic sphere to further expand its territory and gain political power.

An analysis of the course curriculum reveals three overlapping themes that shaped the ways in which the women were introduced and incorporated into the United States. First, an emphasis on women's reading and intellect runs throughout the course. In addition to household management, an American housewife was expected to possess the intellectual prowess to engage with her husband and influence her children. Equally important, she was also expected to be a good companion to her husband, taking great interest in her husband's work, "but never mak[ing] the mistake of telling him how it should be done." After all, "her primary role in life [was] being [her] husband's helpmate."[28] The Japanese housewife was also expected to be a devoted mother. In her downtime, when she was not caring for her children or attending to her chores, she was expected to "read good books and belong to a women's club of which there are many kinds, to try to further her own education so that she may keep up with her children." Finally, the bride school curriculum emphasized the women's "contribution to America." As an immigrant woman entering the US, she had to prove herself worthy of the American people represented by the bride school instructors. To do this, she had to demonstrate strong, moral character as both wife and mother.[29]

Bride schools were not simply home economics taken abroad. They were part of a deliberate effort to strengthen the alliance between the US and Japan while increasing American authority in Asia. The American Red Cross bride schools were part of a network of humanitarian aid organizations that collaborated with the state to extend and strengthen the reach of the United States in the aftermath of World War II.[30] By relying on the work of independent humanitarian organizations like the Red Cross, the United States created a "massive hybrid welfare state" that stretched far beyond the continental US, which was "a critical part of America's rise to a position of global superpower."[31] Preparing Japanese women to be American housewives was one way that the US exercised soft power abroad in the postwar years. However, the network was not unidirectional. Social service agencies in the United States provided information to the bride schools based on their experience working with Japanese women who had already arrived stateside. Several years after the first bride school was underway, the International Institute of San Francisco interviewed one hundred Japanese women in the San Francisco Bay Area who had married American servicemen to better understand the needs of the women and their families in adjusting to American life. The report was shared with American Red Cross bride schools throughout Japan, and excerpts of the report were published in *Fujin Kōron*, a Japanese women's magazine.[32]

Though Japanese brides were the pupils, and American women the instructors, the schools were sites of an exchange of information and knowledge on both sides. Red Cross workers and volunteers described the bride schools as a "*community* project [emphasis in the original]" that increased an international understanding of goodwill between the US and Japan.[33] As the Chairman of Volunteers in the Yokohama field offices explained in 1956, "This is not all one-sided education, believe me, because most of the [American] women who participated said they had gained much in understanding of the Japanese people."[34] Mrs. Johnstone, a Red Cross volunteer and instructor, further explained, "We teach the brides as much as we can of America and its customs. To do an understanding job, we in turn have to learn many valuable things about the Japanese ways of living. We hope the girls don't leave all of their customs behind them."[35] Ultimately, the bride schools were a reciprocal endeavor of knowledge gathering, wherein both parties, student and teacher, learned from one another. Further, as Johnstone's comment reflects, while the brides were encouraged to adopt American style domesticity, they were also encouraged to maintain some aspects of their cultural heritage that Americans might perceive as charming and quaint.

Making Model Citizen-Wives

As time went on, and American men and Japanese women continued to marry in significant numbers, many of those working closely with the state began to view their interracial and transnational marriages as an intimate manifestation of the US-Japan alliance. In a welcome address given at the bride school at Camp Zama, Haru M. Reischauer shared her own story of marrying an American man, hoping her story would ease any reservations the Japanese brides in attendance had. Haru was the

Japanese wife of Edwin O. Reischauer, a widower and the US Ambassador to Japan between 1961–1965. The two were introduced by writer James A. Michener and married in 1956. Reischauer concluded her address by expressing to the women that the intimate bonds they had forged with American men had geopolitical implications. Noting the long history between Japan and America, she stated:

> Today you and I are just carrying this relationship a little further. We have an important role to play in international relations and can do much to further better understanding between our two countries. We can do this by being good wives to our husbands, and good mothers to our children, and also by becoming good American citizens bringing something of Japanese culture with us to America.[36]

Their marriage was a testament to the friendly, and close, relationship between Haru's homeland and adopted country. Indeed for Mrs. Reischauer the personal was political. Contemporary observers often noted that Edwin Reischauer's role as US ambassador to Japan was strengthened by his marriage to Haru, for she was "a bridge between East and West."[37] To fortify harmonious relations between the US and Japan, and between husband and wife, Japanese women were expected to be ideal wives and mothers by dedicating themselves to the domestic sphere. Reischauer herself often spoke publicly about her "passion for domesticity."[38] Work outside of the home was never discussed in the bride schools, while the centrality of domestic and reproductive labor was taken for granted.

Reischauer spoke of marriage and citizenship in the same breath as though its linkage were natural. Yet, she also prefaced it by noting, "you may feel some regret in losing your Japanese citizenship. But you will find that you are not losing anything but gaining something because to your Japanese heritage and culture, you will be adding another culture."[39] Reischauer understood the stakes of obtaining American citizenship even as she encouraged the women to seek it. The Japanese Nationality Law of 1950 had made dual citizenship illegal.[40] Though Japanese women did not automatically lose their Japanese citizenship upon marrying American men, if they wished to obtain American citizenship, they first had to renounce their Japanese citizenship.

The women who entered the US before the passage of the McCarren Walter Act of 1952, which abolished the racial quota system of the 1924 National Origins Act, subverted the intended Japanese exclusion embedded in the 1924 act. Soon after their arrival, these women were given a pathway to citizenship, a right denied the thousands of Japanese immigrants who came before them. However, as Ursula Vogel has described, immigration and citizenship through marriage rested upon "legacies of dependence, of prolonged tutelage and submission to the rule of men encapsulated in the history of marriage."[41] Citizenship through marriage produced dependent citizens whose claims to American citizenship were tied to their marital status; specifically, for Japanese women, their state-sanctioned intimate bonds with American men. For those entering after 1952, though marriage was less a legal factor enabling immigration and citizenship, it remained foundational to their social and cultural identity in the US, and served as a powerful tool for maintaining asymmetrical power between husband and wife. In the postwar period, as in the period of the Gentlemen's Agreement, Japanese women were not excluded from the US but instead incorporated into the nation as the subordinates of men.[42]

The study conducted by the International Institute of San Francisco found that many of the women experienced "recurring periods of insecurity partly because of their constant dependence on their husbands." For many of the women interviewed, spousal dependence was exacerbated by poor communication, financial woes, and their husband's excessive drinking. In response, the women would often speak of divorce. In fact, the social worker who conducted the interviews and wrote the report expressed alarm that the women concluded rather quickly that divorce was the only solution. "This readiness to threaten divorce can add to existing marital difficulties just as can the husband's threat of deportation which he may use too readily," she wrote. The husbands of Japanese immigrant women understood what was at stake if they were to divorce. However, for many, the threat of deportation was made in vain. Many of the women took steps to become naturalized citizens soon after their arrival in the US, and after the 1952 Immigration and Nationality Act, as well as the removal of the quota system in 1965, the threat of deportation became increasingly impotent for Japanese women.[43]

The American Red Cross bride schools are notably featured in a *Saturday Evening Post* article from 1952 titled, "They're Bringing Home Japanese Wives."[44] The article documents the activities of the bride schools in Yokohama, beginning with a brief story about an embarrassed young soldier who brings his "black-haired, olive-skinned and obviously frightened" Japanese bride to the Red Cross to inquire about the bride schools because, as he complained, she did not know how to wear a slip. Several photos accompany the article showing the women receiving lessons on makeup application, pie baking, and infant care. The women in the accompanying photographs stand erect, well-groomed, and are seemingly eager to learn. But, as Elena Tajima Creef points out, they "are also depicted as the products of a defeated and somewhat backward postwar nation who are then hopelessly measured against the presumed superiority of the West."[45] A *Post* reader put it more bluntly, referring to the GI's comment about his bride's slip:

> The authors intimated that a Japanese girl was "dumb" because she did not know how to wear a slip. By the same token, all American women are "dumb" who don't know how to put on a kimono . . . (Now, you or I wouldn't consider that a fair statement, would we?) . . .[46]

In addition to being sites of incorporation, the war bride schools, and the media coverage they received, were also sites where Japanese women became the Other in the American imagination. Creef's mother, Chiyohi, who appeared in the *Post* article, is one of three brides standing around a kitchen table participating in a baking lesson led by an American Red Cross worker. The women are learning to bake an apple pie: one woman standing beside Chiyohi is rolling dough with a pin, and red apples and a pie dish rest atop the table in the foreground. The article does not include any of the Japanese women's voices. In fact, the women were not interviewed for the article.[47] Instead, white American Red Cross workers speak for the women, thereby silencing and othering them at once. The representation of Chiyohi in the pages of the *Post* belies the frustration she felt when she finally saw the article herself. "More I read the *Post*, more makes me mad at their writing concerning Japanese brides," she wrote.[48] As a Japanese bride in postwar America, women like Chiyohi were rendered "visible in her invisibility, peculiar

Figure 4.1. Navy Lieutenant Commander and Lutheran Chaplain (far left) facilitating the "Orientation Program for Japanese Nationals (bridesBrides)," to a group of Japanese war brides aboard the *USS General M. M. Patrick* en route to the United States, December 19, 1951. Naval History and Heritage Command.

in her familiarity."[49] Even the title of "war bride" renders the Japanese woman a "permanent novice," never achieving the title of wife, while also serving as a constant reminder of the conflict between the US and Japan, "thereby highlighting her origin as an enemy alien."[50]

In addition to American Red Cross bride schools in Japan, some women received training en route to the United States. In December 1951, Lieutenant Commander and Lutheran Chaplain, Edwin Andrews, organized what he called an "Orientation Program for Japanese Nationals (Brides)," aboard the *USS General M. M. Patrick*. The program consisted of four lectures, each followed by a screening of a film, and, in some instances, a small group discussion. Andrews began the orientation by first addressing popular (mis)representations of the United States, warning the women that the vast majority of the US was not as it was depicted in Hollywood films. Like the Red Cross bride schools, he encouraged the women to take up opportunities for self-improvement such as taking courses in cooking, typing, sewing, and joining women's clubs and Parent-Teacher Associations. Throughout the four lectures, he insisted the women should speak English, even if done poorly, to combat any hostility they might encounter in the US. He also encouraged them to join a Christian church, as it would further facilitate their belonging in the community. The topic that came up the most in Andrews's lectures was the question of the American people's acceptance of the Japanese brides, as many of the women expressed concern about how they might be perceived in the United States, yet Andrews had no easy answer. He began the orientation by warning the women that they might encounter hostile Americans who may even insult them, but he explained, "it will be much better to make [them] believe you never heard the remark." By the end of the program, Andrews had made a significant effort to reassure the women that Americans would not hate them.[51]

"Good Wife, Wise Mother" (American Style)

To a great degree, the American Red Cross bride schools were an enactment of the prewar Japanese view of women's intended role within the family and nation-state. The "good wife, wise mother" (*ryōsai kenbo*) ideology, which dated back to the pre-WWII era, "defined women's contribution to the progress of the nation to be their labor as 'good wives' and 'wise mothers' in the private world of the home."[52] In exchange, women became members of the modern state. "Good wives, wise mothers" ideology was not only a relic of Imperial Japan: a closer look reveals that the prewar Japanese vision of a woman's role within the family—both the family unit and nation—had much in common with the Cold War United States. In fact "good wife, wise mother" (*ryōsai kenbo*) ideology was not distinctly Japanese, as many developed nations had turned toward the home to embed women in the nation-state, a process of "national assimilation."[53] The women featured in the *Post* article undoubtedly had encountered notions of "good wife, wise mother" prior to the war, and through the American Red Cross bride schools, the good wife and wise mother was transformed into the "model minority bride," an immigrant woman of Asian descent and foreign bride who, in the

American imagination, represented the possibility of ideal domesticity in the postwar years.[54]

The bride schools promoting the "American way of life" were an early element of the anti-communist campaign by the US during the Cold War. The photo of Chiyohi and others in the *Post* predates the infamous "kitchen debate" between Vice President Richard Nixon and Soviet premier Nikita Khrushchev in 1959. In defending American democracy, Nixon extolled consumerism and domesticity as the means to fulfillment. Celebrating the distinct gender roles for men and women, standing in the model American kitchen at the exhibit in Moscow, he pointed to the suburban home equipped with modern appliances as the pinnacle of American democracy. In both the "kitchen debate" of 1959 and the *Post* article on the bride schools in 1952, the American kitchen was the site where democracy via domesticity was achieved, serving an important function in the making of Japanese war brides into good wives and wise mothers, as well as serving the larger ideological struggles of the Cold War.[55]

Additionally, the bride schools established in the United States expanded to bring together brides from Korea and parts of Europe—Czechoslovakia, France, Germany, Poland, and Scotland—as well. In 1953 the American Red Cross reported that the first bride school in the United States was organized at Fort Dix, New Jersey. According to the Red Cross, the class was a success, having graduated "forty-one foreign born wives" of military personnel. Just as in the bride classes in Japan, the women were taught American domesticity in an effort to prepare them for the work of a modern American housewife.[56] According to organizers, the classes were such a success that they were to be replicated on other military bases across the country. Thus, the American Red Cross bride schools in Japan laid the foundation for a global network focused on the domestic training of foreign wives.

Playing House: Portrayals of Japanese Women's Domesticity in Film

After World War II, American interest in Asia was driven by US expansion policy as part of the anticommunist efforts of the Truman administration. However, before Americans could fully support

US foreign policy in Asia, they had to first be persuaded to do so at home. As Christina Klein has explained, the "Cold War was as much of a domestic endeavor as a foreign one."[57] Accordingly, American middlebrow intellectuals propagandized the threat of a communism in Asia to gain support for US containment policies. Japanese war brides married to American GIs were part of the larger narrative that sought to secure widespread support of the Cold War alliance between Japan and the US because their relationship was "the most intimate manifestation of 'international relations.'"[58] Acting strategically, Cold War intellectuals—writers, journalists, filmmakers, teachers, and government officials—championed the United States as a beacon of racial tolerance and big brother to the downtrodden and defeated Japanese Empire. From their perspective, the US conquered Japan in a bout between good and evil, marched in, occupied, and saved the Japanese from self-ruin. As the United States was heading into a conflict with the communist superpowers in North Korea and the Soviet Union, a timely alliance between the US and Japan was to be forged, and Japanese war brides in the American imagination came to represent the possibilities of that alliance. Yet Americans' shift in attitude towards the Japanese came at a high cost. Postwar public discourse about the Japanese and Japanese Americans "assumed two 'natural' or universally recognized hierarchical relationships—man over woman and adult over child."[59] The postwar image of the Japanese in American eyes was one that was simultaneously feminizing and infantilizing, and thus justified the American occupation. Japanese women were at the center of much of this ideological construction, as were the interracial relationships between Japanese women and American men that emerged from the ashes of the war.

While the bride schools, both in Japan and the US, were part of a larger effort to mold the image of Japanese women as wives and mothers into acceptable racial others, images of the women conveyed several conflicting meanings to ordinary Americans. As Caroline Chung Simpson has argued, "The Japanese war bride briefly, but significantly emerged in the mid-1950s as an early form of the model minority Asian American; she was granted the privilege of American identity and even inclusion in the suburban world it inhabited, but for the price of covering and erasing other racial threats and promising not to assert a political voice." In the popular press, the presence of Japanese women married to American servicemen after the war strategically rendered invisible the 120,000 Japanese Americans who were incarcerated during the war. Popular discourse on Japanese war brides mitigated postwar white American anxieties about racial desegregation and Japanese internment during the war. Americans cast their gaze towards the Japanese women and applauded their seemingly successful integration while ignoring the momentous events occurring across the country that proved Americans had a long way to go towards full racial inclusion.[60] Taken together, the bride schools along with US State Department propaganda and America's Cold War obsession with the East created a milieu in which Japanese war brides became a symbol of ideal postwar domesticity, as well as the model minority.

The political deployment of the image of the Japanese woman as an American bride is vividly illustrated in the 1957 Hollywood film, *Sayonara*. Based on the 1953 James Michener novel of the same name, the film portrays the love story of Major Lloyd "Ace" Gruver—an American Air Force pilot—and Hana-Ogi—a Japanese woman—who fall in love in Japan during the Korean conflict.[61] Like the novel, the film opened to great acclaim. Director Joshua Logan cast contemporary heartthrob Marlon Brando, a "Hollywood icon of American masculinity," and Miiko Taka—a Japanese American Nisei—as the lovesick Major "Ace" Gruver and Hana-Ogi.[62]

Set in 1951 Japan, *Sayonara* tells the story of Major Gruver's transformation through his love affair with a Japanese woman. Initially Gruver is opposed to the interracial mingling of American servicemen and Japanese women. When his friend and comrade Sergeant Kelly announces that he is in love with Katsumi, a Japanese woman, Gruver tries to dissuade him. Despite his opposition, Gruver agrees to act as a witness to Kelly and Katsumi's marriage ceremony when they married under fierce opposition from Kelly's commanding officer. Major Gruver's opposition begins to wane, however, when he encounters the beautiful Hana-Ogi. Gruver, who was once uneasy about the cultural differences between the Japanese and Americans, begins to learn Japanese and expresses a new interest in Japanese culture—at one point in the film, he even wears a kimono. Hana-Ogi and Gruver begin a clandestine affair but are eventually discovered. Major Gruver's commanding officer threatens to send him back to the States. A series of dramatic events take place, and it seems as though Major Gruver and Hana-Ogi's relationship will not survive.

Meanwhile, Sergeant Kelly receives orders to return to the States, but he is restricted from bringing a now-expecting Katsumi to America because US immigration law restricted Japanese nationals from entering. Kelly knows that this is an act of sabotage intended to tear him away from Katsumi. He appeals to his commanding officer but is denied. The forlorn lovers—Sergeant Kelly and Katsumi—decide to take their own lives rather than be torn apart. The tragic ending of Kelly and Katsumi's lives serve as a foil to that of Major Gruver and Hana-Ogi. Though both couples face resistance from the United States military, the former is unable to escape the opposition. Soon after Kelly and Katsumi's suicide, special legislation is passed allowing the Japanese wives of American servicemen to immigrate to the United States. Upon hearing this, Gruver rushes to Hana-Ogi and asks for her hand in marriage. The film ends when the two announce their engagement to the press.

Sayonara is a tale of the tragedy and triumph of interracial intimacies between Japanese women and American serviceman, which reflected American anxiety about race relations and the future of American democracy at home and abroad.[63] In the US, the civil rights movement called into question the hypocrisy of racial inequality in a democratic society. The film *Sayonara* was released just three years after *Brown v. Board of Education* ordered the end of racial segregation in the American South, yet what racial integration would look like remained to be seen. Hollywood "sensationalized domestic racial tensions by transposing them onto the less threatening sphere of white-Asian rather than white-African American relations, and [in doing so] showed itself to be a champion of American 'freedom.'"[64]

Furthermore, *Sayonara* reflected anxiety about gender roles as post-WWII America struggled to revert to prewar standards of gender relations. Heterosexual patriarchy loomed over the images of Japanese brides that proliferated after the war, positioning the women in traditional gender roles. In the same year that *Sayonora* was released, another film depicting interracial Japanese and American intimacy hit theaters. *Japanese War Bride*, directed by King Vidor, takes place almost entirely in the United States, when US Army Lieutenant Jim Sterling (played by

Don Taylor) and his Japanese war bride, Tae Shumizu (played by Shirley Yamaguchi), arrive in Jim's hometown of Salinas, California.[65] Upon arriving in the US, the couple is greeted by friendly and helpful faces, as well as some hostile ones.

Throughout the film, Jim's sister-in-law, Fran, who has romantic feelings for him, causes trouble for the couple. Fran's hostility comes to a climax when she writes an anonymous letter accusing Tae of having an affair with the Nisei neighbor, Shiro Hasagawa. Upon hearing the news, Jim lashes out at Tae. Devastated by the false rumors, Tae runs off with their newborn baby to the Hasagawas. Soon after, Fran's actions are revealed, and Jim takes off to find Tae. He finds her at the Hasagawa's cousin's home in the coastal town of Monterey. When Jim finds Tae sitting along the edge of a cliff, she runs away to escape him. A dramatic pursuit ensues. For a moment it seems Tae will escape the burdens of domesticity wrapped up in the prescribed gender role she embodies. When she comes upon a narrow cliff, she has nowhere else to run. She looks down at the sea and, for a brief moment, contemplates jumping. She does not, and instead is swept into Jim's arms. Though the threat of suicide haunts their relationship, in the end the lovers are reunited in a triumphant turn of events. In the film, Gina Marchetti observes "The myth of the subservient Japanese woman attempted to shore up a threatened masculinity in light of American women's growing independence during World War II."[66] *Japanese War Bride* thus ends with the reaffirmation of Tae's domesticity. Filmic representations created within the milieu of what Christina Klein calls "Cold War Orientalism" offer a meditation on the theme of tragedy and triumph in interracial relationships, where death is the only alternative to an otherwise harmonious domestic life. The lesson learned from *Sayonara* and *Japanese War Bride* is that Japanese wives must be strong enough to face resistance or succumb to death, not unlike the tragic end of *Madame Butterfly*.[67]

Portrayals of marriages between American servicemen and Japanese women were not only part of fictional Hollywood representations: the US military also had their hand in producing and circulating stories of American men and Japanese women. In 1952 the US Army produced a short film titled, *Japanese Bride in America*, documenting the story of Miwako, a Japanese woman who marries a man named Walter Lutz, an American serviceman, in Japan and moves to the US shortly after.

Japanese Bride in America was produced by the Civilian Affairs Division under the US Department of War, and in collaboration with the private production company, Knickerbocker Productions. The Civilian Affairs Division was part of a network of government and nongovernment agencies, including the military and film industry, that worked closely together to promote the American way of life in the Cold War era. According to the National Archives, the film was likely created for Japanese women and their families.[68] Indeed, the film was shown to students attending the bride schools.

There are no actors in *Japanese Bride in America*. Instead, the film used real people to depict their personal stories on camera. Most of the film centers on Miwako's struggle to adjust to her new life in Cleveland, Ohio, and like the fictional films of Hollywood, portrays the initial hardships faced by Miwako and Walter.[69] Yet over time, the wrinkles in Miwako's adjustment (such as a language barrier and shyness) are ironed out. As in the fictional accounts, the audience is led to believe that Miwako eventually adjusted to the American way of life and lived "happily ever after" with Walter in Ohio.

The Radtkes Redux

In November 1951, Thomas and Mitsuko Radtke arrived in the United States on furlough to meet Thomas's parents.[70] While in Chicago, the local press took great interest in the young couple, for the elder Radtkes were well known in their Lakeview neighborhood and often shared accounts of Thomas and Mitsuko's ordeal with neighbors. While in Chicago, the young couple was interviewed for the *Chicago Tribune*. Accompanying the story is a photo of Thomas Radtke carrying Mitsuko in his arms across the threshold of his home. Both husband and wife don large smiles that reveal a slight uneasiness. Another photo shows Mitsuko sitting on Thomas's lap, a parent on each side. The photo, ostensibly staged to convey that Mitsuko was "welcomed with open arms into the Andrew Radtke family home," reveals Mitsuko's elevated and prized status, as she sits slightly above the others, her hands clasped in theirs. The Radtkes' embrace of Mitsuko devours her small frame—she is both overwhelmed and outnumbered. After the furlough ended, the young Radtkes returned to Japan but eventually settled in Las Vegas, Nevada.

Conclusion

The second wave of Japanese women's immigration occurred decades after the first picture brides entered the United States. They arrived in a country reshaped by war, Japanese American incarceration, and at a moment when the future of American democracy was unclear. However, the channels by which both streams of women arrived remained the same. Japanese war brides arrived as wives just like their predecessors who arrived after the Gentlemen's Agreement of 1908. For the women who entered after the war, the experiences of immigration

Figure 4.2. "Japanese war bride is welcomed with open arms into the Andrew Radtke family home. Thomas Radtke, 26, holds his bride, Mrs. Mitsuko Ito Radtke, 24, on his lap as his mother and dad sit at either side. The couple is home on 30-day rotation furlough from Japan, where they were married, Dec. 2, 1950," *Chicago Tribune*, November 1951.

and citizenship were a constant negotiation between privilege and subordination. The making of Japanese America was made possible by the privileging of wives in US immigration policy and the ideas of women's—particularly Japanese—domesticity embedded in such policies. The relationship between domesticity and immigration was made clear in the American Red Cross bride schools held throughout Japan. The schools laid the foundation for the mass movement of thousands of Asian women across the Pacific after the Second World War, when the number of women migrating to the US began to outnumber men. This gendered experience of immigration and settlement has profoundly shaped the making of postwar America.

5

Goodwill Ambassadors

Japanese War Brides in Postwar America

On a chilly Friday in November 1953, twenty-four-year-old Etsuko Britton—a young Japanese mother of two living in Chicago—wrapped a silk scarf around her young son's neck and strangled the two-year-old to death. She then wrapped a cord around her own neck. Etsuko was the wife of William Britton, an Air Force sergeant and Chicago native. The two met in Japan just after the end of World War II. Before long they were married and had two children, Charles Jr. and Louise, and made their way to the States where they settled temporarily with Britton's parents on the Northwest Side of Chicago. Soon after their arrival, however, William Britton was called to duty in Korea and left his young bride and two children in the care of his parents. While William was away, Etsuko suffered abuse at the hands of her in-laws. According to Etsuko, her father- and mother-in-law taunted and degraded her with threats and racial slurs. The abuse proved too much for Etsuko, and on November 13, 1953, she took her young son's life and attempted to take her own. When interviewed after her arrest, Etsuko lamented, "I am very lonely." She described the "differences" that she and her in-laws encountered: "All the time they tell me, 'This is not your baby. This my son's baby.' They tell me they send me back to Japan. That I no speak English. I say all the time, 'Very sorry, very sorry—please teach me.'"[1]

Etsuko had attempted *boshi-shinju*, the Japanese practice of mother-child suicide. Tragically for Etsuko and her family, the inability to express herself in English, her husband's departure, and the bullying from her in-laws made her desperate. Etsuko once again tried to commit suicide while in a holding cell in the Cook County jail. During her trial, the press regularly commented on her demeanor and small frame, noting she was 4 foot 10 inches tall and all of eighty-nine pounds. They described her as remorseful and stoic during the whole ordeal.[2] Etsuko's experience reveals the difficulty many Japanese war brides faced in America. In Japan, idealized motherhood, masculine dominance, and domesticity in the nuclear family have historically restricted women's lives, leading some to turn to acts of filicide.[3] In the US, immigrant women whose very belonging rested on their maternal and domestic abilities, endured constraints all the more severe. Not all women were successful students of the American way of life—some, like Etsuko, were isolated and vulnerable. After being convicted of manslaughter, Etsuko was sent back to Japan, leaving her young daughter to be raised by her paternal grandparents, the very ones who had caused Etsuko so much distress.[4]

A Tale of Two Cities

Although the interracial couples in *Sayonara*, *Japanese War Bride*, and *Japanese Bride in America* lived happily ever after, off-screen, the lives of Japanese war brides reveal a more complicated story. Initially, some Americans were hostile to the young wives. Etsuko Britton's in-laws are a case in point. However, unlike the senior Mr. and Mrs. Britton, many Americans quickly learned to tolerate the presence of the young women, if not wholeheartedly welcome them into American life. The presence of Japanese war brides in American homes and in mainstream publications symbolized the connections being made overseas between the once-warring nations.[5]

Japanese war brides' Cold War imagery is notably observed in the iconic portrait of Sachiko Pfeiffer in a 1955 *LIFE* magazine feature.[6] The story of Sachiko Pfeiffer and her marriage to a white American GI and Chicago native, Frank Pfeiffer, is the emblematic representation of Cold War Orientalism. The feature entitled "Pursuit of Happiness by a GI and a Japanese," written by James Michener, author of *Sayonara*, portrays the Pfeiffers as a unique but happily-married couple who had overcome great obstacles in the name of love. Michener details the discrimination Sachiko experienced when first arriving to Chicago in December 1948. He then moves to focus on Sachiko's transformation from foreign bride to American housewife while highlighting the decreasing prejudices of those around her, ending with an American tale of tolerance and triumph.

Upon their arrival to Chicago, the Pfeiffers moved in with Frank's mother, Esther, but soon left after she grew hostile towards Sachiko. The couple moved into their own apartment in the city, but once again Sachiko faced discrimination, this time from her neighbors. Finally, the couple moved to suburban Chicago where, despite the initial hesitation of some white neighbors, they were overwhelmingly welcomed. While Michener highlights the discrimination Sachiko experienced in her first years in the US, more importantly, he focuses on Sachiko's American transformation. It is only when Sachiko is finally able to accept the kindness of her white neighbors that she becomes a full American.

After giving birth to her second child, Sachiko's new neighbors host a surprise baby shower for her, replete with enough gifts to clothe her infant son for an entire year. Although her new neighbors in suburban Chicago had bestowed other acts of kindness upon Sachiko, the surprise baby shower was the turning point in her transformation from Japanese bride to American housewife. According to Michener, "it was only after the baby was born that the little Japanese girl fully comprehended the love in which her neighbors held her. It was then, one might say, that she became an American." In his portrayal, Michener paints an idyllic portrait of the Japanese-American union between Sachiko and Frank Pfeiffer, one where the Japanese bride of the American serviceman overcomes adversity and becomes the quintessential postwar housewife.[7] Her presence is further validated once she gives birth to a second American-born child.

Japanese War Brides as Goodwill Ambassadors

Scene, a Japanese American magazine with a short run in the postwar era, also portrayed a mostly romanticized view of the unions between Japanese war brides and American servicemen. Many of the *Scene* articles featuring Japanese war brides as model American housewives predated those in the popular press. In May 1950, *Scene* featured a small piece under its SceneFlash section titled "Lobbying for Love." The story introduces Carrol Klotzbach, an American serviceman, and his Japanese wife, Mitsue Shigeno. Later on, the Klotzbachs would become familiar faces in *Scene's* collection of war bride stories. In this early feature, husband and wife provided their very own stories documenting their union.[8]

In the meantime, "Lobbying for Love" briefly acquainted readers with the Klotzbachs's tale of love and legislation. While Carrol Klotzbach was stationed in Tokyo, he met the "pretty[] Mitsue Shigeno, a 24-year-old, Tokyo-born girl" twenty-five years his junior. The two fell in love and before long were engaged to be married. However, despite the Alien Brides Act of 1947, Mitsue was considered ineligible for citizenship under US immigration law and was thus restricted from immigrating to the US. She belonged to the group of racially undesirables outlined in the 1924 National Origins Act. But that didn't stop the love-stricken and determined Carrol. As a man of valor (or so the article posits), he lobbied Congress on behalf of Mitsue and, on Valentine's Day 1950, was granted permission to bring her to the United States. The couple married in Washington, DC soon afterwards. A photo appears alongside their story, in which Mitsue is wearing a traditional Japanese kimono, at her husband's request.

A year later, the newlyweds were again featured in *Scene* in a July 1951 article titled, "My Japanese Wife." Mitsue Shigeno, now known as Mrs. Klotzbach, graced the cover with a large and friendly smile. Written by her husband, the article describes Mitsue's adjustment to life in America. His words are striking. First, he equates his wife to a rare Japanese import procured "not by cash or a want ad" but rather by his very own legislative efforts:

> Someone has said that an ideal existence—a heaven on Earth—would be living in an American house, having a Chinese cook and being married to a Japanese Girl. Anyone can manage the house given sufficient cash, and a want ad would procure a Chinese cook. The Japanese wife, however, is unobtainable by either means. It has required special laws and dispensations even after some lovely Plum Blossom has agreed it would be a nice idea. By a Japanese wife is meant the variety indigenous to the home islands of Japan and available only by import.[9]

As the bride of an American serviceman, Mitsue had become the prized possession of Klotzbach—his wartime souvenir. Klotzbach effectively reduced Mitsue to a cultural commodity—personal property he received for his service in the military. Moreover, the article serves to educate and inform the magazine's readership of the possibilities of a white and "yellow" union. Klotzbach assures readers that Mitsue is faring well in the US. He brags that she outperforms American-born housewives in many of her domestic duties. Marriage and domesticity legitimized Mitsue's place in the United States. Though the institution of marriage operated as a state apparatus to include Mitsue, providing a pathway to citizenship and all the rights and responsibilities said citizenship entails, her ability to be a good American housewife is what makes her worthy of full inclusion. In Klotzbach's telling, Mitsue is charming and eager, making her both an acceptable and likeable figure. In other words, Mitsue is a model citizen wife.

As depicted in the magazine, Carrol and Mitsue's marriage also serves another purpose. The Chicago-based publication employs the image of the Klotzbachs' wedded bliss and Mitsue's smooth assimilation into mainstream American life to encourage American acceptance of the Japanese during the resettlement years. When Klotzbach reports that many view Mitsue as "Japan's best Goodwill Ambassador," he pointedly articulated the role she—and by extension, other Japanese war brides—had come to occupy in the imaginations of white and Japanese Americans alike. In this strategy, *Scene* is in concert with the mainstream popular press in presenting the Japanese war bride as a symbol of US racial tolerance. But for the Japanese American readership of *Scene* who were incarcerated during the war, more was at stake in the representations of Japanese war brides. As Simpson argues, if "popular representation of Japanese war brides in relations with exclusively white men became screens for the imaging of a successful racial integration in postwar life," then the images of the Japanese war brides on the pages of *Scene* also became screens for the imaging of a successful Japanese integration into mainstream American life.[10]

A month after "My Japanese Wife" appeared on the pages of *Scene*, a Mrs. James Durwin of Chicago wrote in to express her gratitude towards the magazine for printing the "heartwarming" story. She praises the magazine for telling a story that does not revel in the "shortcomings" of the American people: "I have just returned from a trip abroad in areas where our shortcomings, as a people who profess democratic beliefs, are loudly dinned into the ears of millions. I wish that the story of the Klotzbachs . . . could be told to the people of Southwest Asia—and everywhere for that matter." The Klotzbachs, as portrayed in "My Japanese Wife," had reached the hearts of *Scene* readers by positively portraying what was possible for interracial—especially American and Japanese—unions.[11]

While media representations of Japanese war brides stood for the hopeful possibilities of US race relations both at home and abroad, their

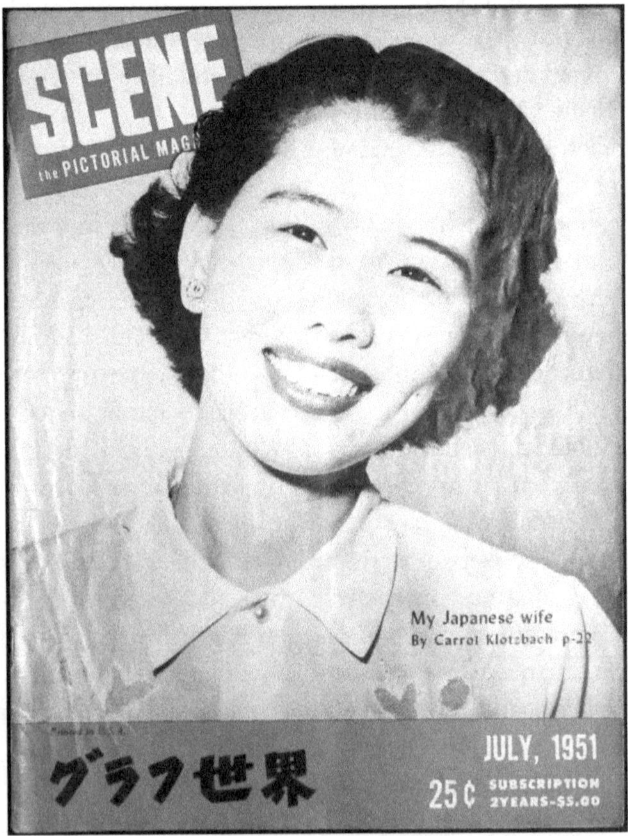

Figure 5.1. "My Japanese Wife," *Scene*, July 1951. Box: 3, Gene Jinye Wakabayashi Papers, 2003.002, JASC Legacy Center, Chicago, IL.

presence in postwar America served to bridge the gap between the post-incarcerated Issei and Nisei. Although the women were in a vulnerable position with very little autonomy away from the home—as in the case of Etsuko Britton—their imaginative presence sheds a positive light on their unions to American men and, in doing so, on Americans of Japanese ancestry in the postwar era.

The Cosmo Club

Once in the United States, many Japanese war brides organized themselves into social clubs in an attempt to negotiate their multilayered identities: Japanese woman and American wife and mother; recent enemy and Cold War ally. In many ways the war bride clubs were an expression of what Vicki Ruiz calls "women's border journeys," the idea that immigrant women and their children travel along many borders "not solely in terms of travel but of internal migration—creating, accommodating, resisting, and transforming, the physical and psychological environs of their 'new' lives in the United States."[12] Like the many immigrant women before them, Japanese war brides traversed many borders, both tangible and abstract.

Further, the clubs were reminiscent of the Nisei women's clubs organized in places along the West Coast. According to Valerie Matsumoto, nisei organizations—particularly those organized and led by urban Nisei women—"provided a key venue in which young urban women could claim modern femininity, an American identity, and public space."[13] The same was true for the war bride clubs of the postwar era. By the mid-1950s, the clubs had become a space for Japanese war brides to carve out a hybrid American identity based on their role as American wives and mothers alongside their Japanese culture—the marriage of which was often flaunted as a mainstay of early Cold War era media. Like the young women Matsumoto writes about, Japanese immigrant women organized as a means to "adjust" to American life by creating a space to assert—and explore—their Japanese American womanhood.

The Cosmo Club was founded in the summer of 1952 under the auspices of the Chicago Resettlers Committee. The purpose of the club was to educate Japanese women on all things American and provide a safe space for the women to socialize in their native tongue with fellow countrymen and women. The club held socials, family outings, and fundraisers to assist the less-fortunate brides who experienced hardship since arriving in the US. Sachiko Pfeiffer, from the 1955 *LIFE* article, served as one of the first co-chairwomen of the club. Believed to be one of the firsts of its kind, the club inspired the founding of many other Japanese war bride clubs around the country, most notably the Fujiyama Society of New York City. There was also the Cherry Blossom Society in Long Beach, California,[14] the Japanese War Bride Club in Albuquerque, New Mexico,[15] and the Fuji Club in Cleveland, Ohio, which had twelve members in 1957.[16] There was also an "ambitious" nationwide plan by Hisako Nagashima Stevens to organize the "Japanese War Brides Club of America" from her Mansfield, Ohio home.[17]

At its inception, the Cosmo Club had twenty members. Two years later, the club officials boasted about having forty members, more than any other club of its kind.[18] Under the auspices of the Resettlers Committee, the club functioned as a site for cultural construction. It was a place where the war brides were able to construct a new identity for themselves based on negotiations between their Japanese heritage and their new American life. In 1952 the women participated in the annual Christmas festival sponsored by the Museum of Science and Industry in Chicago. Cast as representatives of the Japanese community, the war brides were responsible for decorating the festival's "Japanese Christmas Tree."[19] Indeed the festival presented an opportunity for the women to publicly display their Japanese otherness while embracing Christian American cultural practices. Like marginalized women before them, Japanese war brides became nonpolitical diplomats to the larger white community of Chicago.[20]

Along with their benefactors at the Resettlers Committee, the clubwomen saw it fit to change the club's name as they grew in members and prestige. A year after its founding, the club put out an open call to the community eliciting suggestions for a new name. Executive Director of the Committee Kenji Nakane stated that the clubwomen were searching for a new name that was more appropriate than "War Bride Club," one that would "emphasize the club's cosmopolitan feel." The club offered four prizes to those who could come up with the best names, and by the end of 1953, the Japanese War Brides Club of Chicago had become The Cosmo Club.[21]

The Cosmo Club, as Nakane and others put it, was a more attractive name that showed the women to be true "cosmopolites." After all, they were the lucky ones, for "the men they married in Japan called Chicago home."[22] Indeed, the women of the club were by and large the lucky ones. Unlike Etsuko Britton and other brides who experienced tremendous hardship when they arrived in the United States, the "cosmopolites" were probably the most supported of their peers. These women found friendship and belonging within the club. They were closely tied to the Resettlers Committee, which meant that they were surrounded by people of Japanese ancestry with whom they shared a common racial and cultural heritage. Moreover, the "cosmopolites" found themselves in a place of influence as their marriages to white men—and in some cases Nisei servicemen—allowed them a degree of respect and admiration as the wives of the Greatest Generation.

Soon after adopting the title of Cosmo Club and transforming themselves from war brides (a name that frequently had negative connotations) to the more sophisticated "cosmopolite," the women began an earnest campaign to aid their downtrodden sisters. The clubwomen worked tirelessly to make small handcrafts—presumably Japanese handcrafts—to be sold at a local Chicago bazaar. Most of the proceeds were used to help other war brides who fared less well. In addition, they held two talent shows to raise money for their less fortunate countrywomen. The shows were a success. The "bustling clubwomen" also built up a well-used library, hosted dances, poetry sessions, and potlucks where "the cold buffet was Japanese. The hot food was Chinese. The whiskey was American and Scotch."[23] Chicago war brides in the Cosmo Club seemed to be adjusting well to their new environment. Serving as local cultural ambassadors, committee members often boasted of the hard work and success of the club, especially its work in aiding war brides who found themselves in dire straits.

However, in their work as ambassadors, Cosmo Club members made little issue of their racial status. They often displayed their Japaneseness for the benefit of others but made little to no reference of the discrimination many endured. In 1954, *Scene* ran an article entitled "Are War Brides

Happy?" in an effort to address widespread concern that the brides were experiencing hard times in the US. One bride told *Scene* that "[she] was most happy and America [had] presented no "racial problems" to [her]."[24] The article answered the title question with a loud and firm yes. While women like Etsuko suffered, their "lucky" sisters downplayed the racial hostilities of the day.[25]

In order to fulfill their role as "Goodwill Ambassadors," war brides had to put on a face that showed others they were doing just fine in the US, lest they reveal the ambivalent and delicate circumstances of the Japanese in postwar America. In "Are War Brides Happy?" *Scene* explicitly de-emphasized this potential problem, assuring readers that the "the matter of 'race' is in many instances exaggerated. 'Language' has place, but, like 'race,' it has been elevated to a rank that outstrips the true facts."[26] According to the article, Japanese-American unions were far from unique. Rather, these couples were like any other newlyweds in America and faced a similar set of challenges. Race and language were exaggerations that obscured the very ordinariness of the war bride marriages. By downplaying the racial otherness of Japanese war brides and the unique quality of their marriages, war brides and *Scene* writers alike tried to cast off the foreignness associated with the Japanese women and instead highlight the ways that they were just like other Americans.

In addition, some Japanese women looked to the war bride clubs as an opportunity to "sell democracy" to both Americans and the Japanese. Hisako Nagashima Stevens, the bride who planned to organize the Japanese War Brides Club of America, told reporters in 1952 that she wanted to organize a national club of Japanese war brides to "sell democracy to the people of Japan."[27] Stevens believed that as the wife of an American man, she had a lot to teach her brothers and sisters in Japan. Indeed, selling democracy became a task for Kyoko Batchelor, the wife of Corporal Claude Batchelor.

After being captured by Korean forces and held in a prisoner of war camp in 1952, Claude Batchelor defected and joined the Communist struggle. After the Korean War ended, Batchelor refused to return to the United States. Batchelor sympathized with the North Koreans who pointed out the hypocrisy of the United States—a nation of abundance who "neglected its poor people . . . especially its Negro people."[28]

Batchelor's young Japanese wife, Kyoko, wrote him regularly pleading for his return. After some time, Batchelor was convinced and sought repatriation. Upon his return to Tokyo, Batchelor was reunited with Kyoko, expressing regret for having disgraced his country. He vowed to fight communism for the rest of his life.[29] However, after legal proceedings, Batchelor was sentenced to twenty years hard labor, though he ultimately served only one-and-a-half years.[30]

Lost in much of the contemporary media coverage and literature is the role Kyoko played in Batchelor's return. From her home in Tokyo, Kyoko played a significant role in Claude's return to democratic ideals. In 1954 Batchelor explained to the press that it was Kyoko's undying love that finally persuaded him to come back—so much so that Batchelor asked Kyoko to write his comrades and fellow defectors still in North Korea in an effort to persuade them as well.[31] Batchelor's story captivated the nation during the early years of the Cold War as a modern turncoat-turned-patriot, and it was Kyoko, Batchelor's Japanese wife, who sold American-style democracy to Claude, ultimately persuading him to leave the North Korean camp and return home.[32]

In post-World War II United States, popular discourse in film and the media as well as US state propaganda created a world wherein Japanese women as brides to American servicemen were not only tolerated but championed as a symbol of US-Japan relations in the geopolitical climate of the Cold War. These interracial unions also ostensibly embodied racial tolerance in the United States in the emerging civil rights movement. Portraits of interracial couples like the Pfeifers and Klotzbachs as well as the fictional unions seen in film reveal more about the creators than the subjects, and "[w]hether they liked it or not, the personal became the political for interracial couples in 1950s America."[33] But before Japanese women could become symbols of Cold War domesticity, they first had to be groomed into ideal American housewives. This process started before they arrived in the US. Once in the US, Japanese war brides organized themselves in an effort to negotiate their new status as American wives and mothers. But the representational value assigned to Japanese women was only extended to those women who married white servicemen. Likewise, the cherry blossom clubs that emerged in the fifties often restricted membership to women who had married white men. The Japanese women who married African American servicemen

Figure 5.2. The Cosmo Club, Chicago circa 1950. From left to right: Kenji Nakane, Naoko Taketani, Emiko Takada, Kiyoko Castellanoz, Fusako Johnson, Sayo Kirkland, Tsuyuko Rosengren, Corky Kawasaki, Toshiko Selby. Group 10, Japanese American Service Committee Collection, Chicago, IL.

were less likely to be seen as the model minority brides so valued during the Cold War era.

"The Loneliest Brides in America"

In January 1953, *Ebony* magazine featured an article titled, "the Loneliest Brides in America" explaining how the Japanese women who married Black men had not been fully accepted into African American communities nor the growing community of Japanese war brides in the US. It described how white Americans and even Japanese Americans shunned the women. Furthermore, the women interviewed explained how they found it difficult to maintain friendships with other Japanese war brides who married white American soldiers.

Particularly, Japanese women married to Black servicemen were the subject of criticism from African American women. A year earlier, *Ebony* reported that "some US Negro women accuse the Japanese brides of 'spoiling our men' and are hostile to them."[34] Ms. Ethel Jones from

Vallejo, California, wrote in response to an earlier *Ebony* editorial entitled, "The Truth about Japanese War Brides" that "there are some of us that are more kind and considerate than those Japanese girls . . . I'm sure that there are a lot of American girls that could make good wives to servicemen, but you'll only know by giving them a chance. I'd appreciate it if once in a while you'd write a story on 'The Truth About American War Brides.'"[35] While Teruko Shimzu, the wife of James Miller, an African American serviceman, was well received by her in-laws, she found "few colored women as friends."[36] Indeed, to some African American women, the presence of Japanese war brides in their community posed a romantic threat. Much of Black women's animosity was fueled by the Black press who bolstered Japanese women as model wives, while at the same time, undermining Black womanhood.

Despite initial hostility expressed by some Black women, many indeed befriended the Japanese brides. For instance, Anna Jane Atkins wrote to the editor of *Ebony* after the January 1953 article asking; "In what way could I be of aid to these girls who have left their homes to come here, expecting happiness, and finding snobbery?" Atkins ended her short query with an offer to corresponded with the women. Atkins was not alone; several other readers—both men and women—wrote to express their sympathy and willingness to extend friendship with the Japanese women.[37] Black women proved to be central to Japanese women's adjustment to life in postwar America.[38]

Eiko Washayama befriended Kathereen Palmer, a Black neighbor. The women began their friendship during a "back-fence conversation" and eventually began visiting each other's homes. Both women are pictured in the *Ebony* article, standing in what appears to be Eiko's kitchen. The caption reads, "Friendly neighbor Kathereen Palmer shows Eiko Washayam Wigglesworth how to use a gas stove . . . and how to prepare her husband's meals."[39] Despite the hostility of some Black women, most Japanese war brides were ultimately accepted by their African American husband's family, and some like Eiko found friendship with Black neighbors. Though many of the couples did not initially find a community of welcoming arms once in the US, they instead created communities of their own in what *Ebony* called "tiny settlements of Negro-Japanese couples scattered across the US."[40] These "settlements" were typically located in Black urban areas or within close proximity to a military base. Teruko and James Miller found their refuge from the suspicious and hostile world in a neighborhood made up of similar couples located at "the center of Indianapolis' Negro area."[41] Takiko Kondo Tabb met her husband during the Allied Occupation when he was serving in the United States Army. They settled in her husband's hometown of Pittsburgh, Pennsylvania, in a Black working-class neighborhood. When Takiko passed away in 2005, she was laid to rest in Pittsburgh.[42] While in 1953, Japanese war brides had yet to be "freely accepted into Negro communities" and had "received half-hearted welcomes from in-laws," their settlement patterns reveal an underlying tie to Black communities. When a Japanese woman married an American man, she married into the community to which he belonged. For those who married Black servicemen, as mothers of Black children and wives of Black men, Japanese war brides carved out a place for themselves within the larger Black community.

Japanese Women Contest The Black/White Binary

When Setsuko arrived in Dallas, Texas, in 1952 with her husband Eddie, she encountered an unfamiliar world. Eddie's family welcomed her into their home and community. Initially she felt safe, welcomed, and generally at ease, until a series of events forced her to consider her status within the US racial hierarchy. One day Setsuko and her sister-in-law went downtown to watch a film at the local Black movie theater. To her dismay the theater refused to sell Setsuko a ticket. Classifying her as white, the theater feared reprisals for breaking segregation laws. Setsuko was confused because she had never before considered herself white. On another occasion, while shopping and running errands alone, Setsuko wandered into a theater designated for Mexicans and was pleasantly surprised at being admitted. Later, she also found refuge in the local Mexican bingo parlor. But when Setsuko's mother-in-law found out that she had been visiting establishments designated for Mexicans, she scolded her. If Setsuko was to remain a member of the family and community, she had to abide by the strict rules of racial conduct. This meant she was not to mingle with those outside the Black community. For Setsuko this was a hard lesson to learn, but a crucial one in Jim Crow Texas.[43]

During her stay in Dallas, Setsuko experienced the realities of the segregated South. After hearing about several acts of violence committed by whites against both Blacks and Mexicans, Setsuko became alarmed and wondered, "What kind of cowboy do that?"[44] The Western films imported into Japan had significantly influenced her perception of white Americans. As a child she had seen images of heroic cowboys like John Wayne fighting against evil and was disappointed to find that characters were merely fictional. The racial violence that plagued the country and in Dallas particularly troubled her. Until then she had never been homesick, but soon she wished to return to Japan.[45]

Japanese war brides who married Black GIs from Southern states encountered a complex and hostile racial environment. Since most Southerners saw racial differences primarily through a Black and white paradigm, they often tried to fit the Japanese women into this model.[46] Setsuko's experience in Dallas reveals how the Japanese women who married African American servicemen tried to negotiate their racialized existence. She had never considered herself white, and found that being racially classified as such limited her mobility in the Black community. This troubled Setsuko because the Black community was where she and Eddie called home. And though she had never interacted with Mexican people, she was surprised to find, in Jim Crow Texas, that her race had not deterred them from allowing her to patronize their establishments as had the Black theater. The reaction of Setsuko's mother-in-law shows how rigid racial boundaries were not to be taken lightly, especially in the segregated South. By patronizing Mexican establishments, Setsuko unknowingly stepped outside those boundaries.

War brides experienced discrimination at the hands of other Japanese Americans as well. Japanese war brides who married white American GIs also distanced themselves from the war brides who married men of color. This was in large part a decision made on behalf of their white husbands who harbored prejudices against Black Americans. After arriving in the United States, Sumi and Willie Brown and their infant son Michael settled into their new home in the Presidio of San Francisco, where Willie had been stationed. Willie remembered the pain Sumi felt when the Japanese community in San Francisco's Japantown shunned her. Willie explained how happy Sumi was when she learned of Japantown, a place where she could buy Japanese groceries and household items. However, after her first visit to the community, Sumi returned home upset. According to Willie:

> She said that everywhere she went in Japanesetown [as it was called then] that she was made to feel bad, she was greeted with a scowl and treated with scorn. She could not figure out what caused her own country folk to treat her like a hated enemy. . . . They regard folks straight from Japan as if they were the enemy, because most Americans thought of them that way and they were seen as a threat, even to the Japanese folks who were born here. That's because they wanted so much to be looked at as loyal citizens, and they distanced themselves from those folks who couldn't speak English well or acted "too Japanesey."[47]

Sumi's status as a newly-arrived immigrant woman made her the subject of criticism in the well-established Japanese American community of Japantown, San Francisco. When the first Japanese war brides began arriving in the United States in 1947, Japanese Americans were still coming to grips with wartime incarceration. Before Japanese Americans were released from incarceration camps, they were required to take a loyalty questionnaire administered by the War Relocation Authority (WRA). The questionnaires purportedly tested and measured the loyalty of the Japanese to determine if the individual in question deserved to be admitted back into American society. The WRA was primarily concerned with the cultural practices of the Japanese, as engaging in Japanese culture and custom was seen as un-American and thus a disloyal act, according to the WRA. Naturally, many of the incarcerated Japanese made a strident effort to appear as loyal Americans. The "forced cultural assimilation" wrought by the WRA and their loyalty questionnaires prompted many Japanese Americans to shun, or at least minimize, their Japanese heritage.[48] Thus many sought to distance themselves from the newly arrived war brides.[49]

In 1962, the International Institute of San Francisco, a social service agency committed to assisting immigrant groups in the United States, prepared a report on Japanese war brides and their families "in order to discover their needs and relate community services to the needs expressed." The report noted some of the difficulties the women encountered in adjusting to life in America. It specifically noted the antagonisms between the established Japanese American community and the war brides. After interviewing one hundred Japanese war brides in the San Francisco area, the report explained that many of the interviewees had "experienced rejection in one form or another by the Issei and Nisei of the Japanese community."[50] As they struggled to rebuild their lives after the devastation of incarceration, Japanese Americans wished to be seen as Americans first and foremost, and made a significant effort to "assimilate" into American society. In doing so, they consciously eschewed the newly arrived Japanese war brides.

Furthermore, the Japanese American community was also averse to associating with Japanese war brides who married African American men. After Sumi Brown's incident in Japantown, Mac, a family friend and an African American man married to a Japanese woman, asked Willie if Sumi had taken along their young son on her visit to Japantown. Mac laughed when Willie answered yes. Mac explained the racial prejudices that many Japanese Americans harbored towards Black Americans.[51] In 1957, the International Institute of Metropolitan Detroit reported in a conference paper that the "Issei and Nisei, scarcely recovered from their injuries and insults of the war years in relocation camps, express reluctance, for a number of reasons, to associate with Japanese wives, particularly if they have Negro husbands."[52] As newly arrived immigrant women married to African American men, Japanese war brides were a double insult to the Japanese American community. They faced several layers of discrimination stemming not only from their own racial status in the United States, but also from that of their husbands.

In their exhaustive 1962 study, the International Institute of San Francisco reported:

> A common complaint among newly-arrived women is that the early-arrived women are not helpful at all. Newcomers often come to the United States with the expectation that they can easily find friendship and support among the early arrivals. They are very disappointed to find that the "old-timers" among the Japanese wives of Americans in many cases no longer think of themselves as Japanese but Americans and act accordingly. This is especially true among those who have acquired American citizenship.[53]

Referring to the first Japanese war brides to arrive in the United States in the immediate post-WWII years, like Sachiko Pfeiffer, as "old-timers," the study found that after entering the country, these women believed themselves to be fully incorporated into American society. Further, after receiving citizenship status, the "old-timers" drew a line between themselves and the newly-arrived brides. This friction between the "old" and "new" immigrant women reveals some of the internal conflicts that plagued the small war bride communities across the country.

Moreover, Japanese war bride clubs that sprang up around the United States during the first years of the arrival of Japanese war brides (such as the Cosmo Club) excluded war brides who married African American GIs. Despite the good intentions of such clubs, many Japanese war brides who married Black men found that they were not welcome. Between 1955 and 1956, the International Institute of Metropolitan Detroit undertook an extensive study on Japanese war brides in the Detroit area, interviewing ninety women, sixty-one of whom were married to white Americans and twenty-seven of whom were married to Black Americans. The study found that the racial prejudices of the white husbands deeply influenced their wives' interaction with women married to Black men. According to Marian Mizuno, a Japanese-born social worker who worked with the Institute while studying in the US:

> It seems that Japanese brides married to Negroes have an additional emotional burden, because of the prejudices prevailing in the community . . . These Negro-Japanese couples have met some rejection from the Caucasian Japanese couples, who are in one way or another sensitive to the Negro prejudice and refuse to associate with Negroes. It was found that in general the Caucasian husbands did not want their Japanese wives to visit or relate to those Japanese women married to Negroes.[54]

One bride told *Ebony*, "It seems that the Japanese girls who married white soldiers got very high hat when they came to America and drew a color line on us and our husbands."[55] In 1954, another bride married to a white serviceman told researchers in Hawai'i that among her closest war bride friends, the two married to Black men seldom spoke of their husbands. She explained, "My husband has no prejudices against

Negroes but some of the white husbands of the Japanese war brides forbade their wives to associate with the Japanese war brides of Negro men."[56] Once again, Japanese women who married African American servicemen were forced to confront American racial prejudices. Even within the small war bride communities and the more formal war bride clubs, Japanese war brides married to Black men found little support. Elena Creef, the daughter of a Japanese war bride and white GI, notes that the Japanese war bride community of the Pacific Northwest—the largest and strongest community of its kind—is intensely complicated and "painfully splintered along multiple axes of long-term friendships and alliances held together by race and class affiliation."[57]

Setsuko found an enduring friendship with Michiko, another Japanese war bride married to an African American GI.[58] Like Setsuko, Michiko was left to raise her two children alone when her marriage ended in divorce. The two women remained inseparable for years, and when Michiko passed away, leaving behind two small children, Setsuko took it upon herself to raise them. Setsuko's voice began to crack and lose its vigor when she spoke of her dear friend Michiko. This friendship is only one of two that Setsuko spoke of; the other is with a childhood friend who married a white serviceman. Although the two women have not seen each other since their early days in the United States, they still remained in contact via telephone conversations and the occasional holiday or birthday card. Their distant friendship is likely the result of Setsuko's ties to the African American community.

Setsuko eventually left Dallas and moved around the country with her husband Eddie and their two daughters, Lorraine and Mary, eventually settling in Marin City, California.[59] Though millions of African Americans sought new lives in the Great Migration throughout the twentieth century, during World War II, thousands of African Americans migrated from the South to Marin City specifically, where temporary housing had been set up for wartime shipyard workers. Marin City, an unincorporated community in the North San Francisco Bay area, was predominantly Black until recently.[60] Setsuko eventually divorced Eddie after his gambling and womanizing habits took an emotional toll on her. After the divorce Setsuko raised her daughters, in addition to the children of her friend in Marin City, as a single mother. She easily found work in San Francisco Japantown restaurants and in the domestic service industry. Even after her children grew up and moved away, Setsuko remained in Marin City where the vast majority of her neighbors were African American. Setsuko passed away in the summer of 2015.

Japanese war brides and African American servicemen faced a series of obstacles. Although some relationships ended in heartache, others endured for decades. After traveling across the world with her career military husband, Command Sergeant Major Willie Lee Brown, Sumi and Willie settled near Savannah, Georgia and raised four sons together. Willie retired after thirty-five years of active service, and when he passed away in 1997, Sumi returned to Japantown, San Francisco where she stayed until her death in June 2010.[61]

Conclusion

Japanese women's immigration after World War II was facilitated by political maneuvers and personal sacrifices made by American men serving abroad. During the war, the US encouraged civilian worship of the combat soldier, which ultimately led to GI entitlements in the postwar recovery period.[62] The freedom to marry non-American women was "the least we can do for the men who fought our wars overseas. . . ."[63] Yet, for those American men who wished to marry Japanese women excluded by immigration legislation, the freedom to marry would have to bypass racial exclusion. Thus a series of War Bride Acts made Japanese immigration possible once again. In this way, Japanese women "influenced the course of postwar immigration policymaking."[64]

The second wave of Japanese women's immigration occurred decades after the first picture brides entered the US. They arrived in a world shaped by war and the defeat of the Japanese imperial state, all while the US military abroad continued to grow. However, the channels by which both streams of women arrived remained the same. Japanese war brides arrived as wives just like their predecessors who arrived after the Gentlemen's Agreement of 1908. Their presence in the United States was both allowed and legitimated by ideas of women's—particularly

Japanese—domestic labor. As such, the making of Japanese America was made possible by a gendered diaspora that at times privileged women immigrants as wives to Japanese men, and in the postwar era, American men. This gendered experience of immigration and settlement profoundly shaped the making of Japanese America.

Epilogue

World War II marked a turning point in United States immigration law at the same time that it set the stage for a new phase in race and gender relations in America. Racial liberalism took hold in the war years when Americans were confronted with the atrocities committed by Nazi Germany. As many scholars have shown, the 1940s offered exceptional opportunities.[1] The war industry and the subsequent mass movement of people—from the South to the North and West, from rural farms and suburbs to industrialized cities, and from childhood homes to small towns in Europe and islands in the Pacific—created new opportunities for America's racial minorities. It also facilitated encounters between distinct racial groups who had never before interacted on such scale. Though World War II and the 1940s more broadly created unprecedented opportunities, it also revealed a web of contradictions in US policy and practices. While official wartime rhetoric claimed America was fighting for democracy abroad, the practices of racial segregation in the military and the South—and the wartime incarceration of Japanese Americans—made clear that the US had a long way to go to achieve the values it espoused.

The era also witnessed an "opening" of immigration law. The National Origins Act of 1924 brought immigration to a halt when xenophobic immigration policymakers excluded many would-be immigrants because they believed in the superiority of the white race. In 1947, just two years after the end of the war, Japanese women were the first formally excluded group to be permitted to enter the US since 1924. This exception was made not in service of the women, but as an act of goodwill towards the US servicemen they married in Occupied Japan. The McCarran-Walter Act of 1952 lifted the bar on Asian exclusion, providing a pathway to citizenship and unencumbered entry for Asian women who were the wives of US military personnel. However, the Act continued to adhere to most of the quotas outlined in the National Origins Act of 1924. In 1965, the

Hart-Celler Act finally abolished the National Origins Act of 1924. Lost in much of the conversation on postwar immigration legislation are the ways in which women's bodies, particularly Japanese women, served the nation. These women entered as subordinated subjects whose presence fulfilled explicit political agendas. The persistent and stubborn view of Japanese women as Madame Butterflies continued to shape how Americans imagined Japanese femininity. In Cold War America, the Madame Butterfly became the "model minority wife"—the racialized immigrant bride of Asian descent and superior moral character. Some women contributed to this way of thinking by performing Japanese femininity for American audiences. Perhaps they realized that their citizenship was made legitimate through their role as a "good wife, wise mother."

Despite the historical circumstances that permitted Japanese women to enter after the war, their immigration via domesticity was in fact part of a longer history. At the turn of the twentieth century, Japanese women were permitted entry as brides in an era of racial exclusion. But soon after, the same gendered ideals that permitted their entry were used to attack the women and solidify the anti-Japanese agenda of West Coast politicians, resulting in two streams of female migration rarely studied together. While marriage provided a means of inclusion for some Japanese women, it also was a means to exclude the Japanese men who remained unwed. *Picture Bride, War Bride* fills this analytical gap and in doing so reveals how gender—broadly conceived to include masculinity, femininity, sexuality, marriage, and domesticity—fundamentally shaped the Japanese experience in the United States.

Foreign Brides and the Commodification of Intimacy

Since World War II, women have dominated migration flows into the United States. This trend started with the thousands of Japanese war brides who came to America in the immediate postwar years. This is not a phenomenon particular to the US. Across the globe, women have left their home countries in search of better opportunities abroad. Many of the opportunities available to women—especially women from developing nations—reflect "the real and imagined commodification of intimate relations, particularly those involving marriage, sex, and reproductive work." Though the lives of these modern migrant women reflect recent economic and political changes, women's migration has long rested on intimate encounters and the commodified gains such encounters beget. To be sure, commodification does not denote monetary value only. Many tangible opportunities are to be gained. Various relationships, both sexual and nonsexual, are "commodified in terms of material expectations." As Nicole Constable argues, "Commodification may be hidden, disguised, mystified, denied, or reinterpreted as a gift or experienced as liberating and modern."[2]

This fact does not negate the authenticity of these relationships. Indeed, romantic love, arguably the most sacred expression of human bonding, is a social construct. How it takes shape and is expressed varies by context, place, and time. This analysis is not a judgment of the many Japanese women who came to the US as wives. Instead, it aims to take seriously the very real motivating factors that compel people to leave their country of birth and seek life anew. Future studies of war brides would do well to position the migration of women as brides within a longer history of the commodification of intimacy and women's migration.

Legacies

The women who left Japan for America post-World War II gave birth to a new generation of Japanese Americans—one that was decidedly mixed-race. Growing up in the postwar years, the children of war brides and American servicemen experienced racial discrimination. Their lives and experiences warrant further research. Both Setsuko and Sumi's adult children reported some of the daily struggles they encountered, and the nuances of growing up Black Japanese.[3] Setsuko's daughter vividly remembered being teased and taunted in school because of her Japanese heritage. Sumi's son, Anthony Brown, a successful jazz musician in the San Francisco Bay area, described a typical meal in the Brown family home: a mixture of both Southern cooking and Japanese cuisine. For Sumi and Setsuko's children, growing up mixed-race was a constant process of negotiation. In much the same way as the women of the Cherry Blossom Club, they learned to negotiate their racial status in a world that viewed racial experiences through a Black and white lens. Despite their struggles, these families endured, giving rise to new ways of thinking about race-making since World War II.

Indeed, a body of scholarship termed critical mixed-race studies has emerged to explore the experiences of mixed-race Americans. In fact, "the study of multiracial people is the fastest growing segment of ethnic studies."[4] This disciplinary field was born out of the multiracial movement that coalesced around the 1990s campaign to have "multiracial" added to the available racial categories in the 2000 census. Critics of the 1990s census movement have argued that the motives of many of those involved (white mothers of biracial children) were attempting to distance themselves and their children from Blackness and stake a claim in whiteness.[5] Indeed, the 1990s census movement and its critics were focused on the Black and white binary, but the struggle actually dates back to the civil rights era.[6] Moreover, the civil rights movement itself began as a multiracial effort made up of various racialized groups beyond the Black/white binary. In his analysis of the long civil rights movement, Mark Brilliant argues that the predominant understanding that the problem of race was synonymous with the "Negro problem" obscures the history of multiracial alliances and civil rights agitation that took place on the American "racial frontier" of California.[7]

For mixed-Japanese Americans born in the postwar period, the question of racial identity is further complicated because these individuals are not necessarily haunted by the wartime incarceration of their families. Narratives of the war and trauma undoubtedly influence familial dynamics and the experiences of racialization for postwar mixed-Japanese Americans and their descendants, but how these narratives are rendered differently is a question of concern for scholars of Japanese America. Moreover, the children of Black men and Japanese women—what scholars term "dual-minority Americans"—have much to teach about the differential processes of racialization. Such considerations may include how race and power operate in the lives of mixed-race Japanese Americans who are not white, or, how the process of racial identity formation is informed by dual-minority racial status. These lines of inquiry fall within a subfield of critical mixed-race studies that seeks to decenter whiteness.

Jero, born Jerome Charles White Jr., is the first American-born enka singer to achieve success in Japan. Enka, a popular genre of ballad-driven music that emerged in postwar Japan, has been likened to country music in its content and blues in its sound. White is the grandson of Takiko, a Japanese war bride who married a Black serviceman and settled in the United States in the 1950s. Born and raised in Pittsburgh, Pennsylvania, White credits his grandmother for his successful career as an enka singer because it was she who first introduced him to the music of her generation when he was just a child.[8] In interviews, White frequently describes how his Japanese grandmother, who cared for him throughout his childhood, would have her favorite enka records on frequent rotation. Enka was the soundtrack to White's early years, and he began to sing enka ballads to his grandmother when he was five years old.

Much has been made of White's crossover appeal because of his African American racial heritage and Japan's historically fraught relationship with Blackness. Yet, White's success has much to do with the way he expresses his Blackness. White uses his Japanese cultural heritage passed down from his maternal grandmother, Takiko, to give his Japanese audience an "alternative image of African Americans." In short, White embodies and expresses both his Japanese and Black American ancestry in his music and performance, making him a "cross-generational bridge" between the US and Japan.[9] White's crossover success is part of a small but growing visibility of mixed-race Japanese Americans in the entertainment industry.[10] These individuals challenge racial categories in numerous ways, revealing the very tenuous nature of such categories. Examining this alternative image of African Americans that Jero projects in Japan reveals how he uses traditional Japanese forms of cultural production, like enka, to usurp cultural expectations and challenge assumptions about Black modes of expression in Japan.

The presence of mixed-Japanese Americans also speaks to the growth of the US military presence abroad since World War II. Scholars have recently begun to take seriously the historical fact that many mixed-race Americans—particularly those of Asian descent—have intimate ties to the United States military.[11] With a few notable exceptions, scholars are only just beginning to understand the role of the military in the making of mixed-race America.[12] For the many children of war brides from Japan and other parts of Asia and Europe, life was born out of the chaos of war, and military occupation created a legacy of militarism within the private sphere of the family. It is this history that has shamed many women and kept them silent for far too long. Despite this, it is their children and grandchildren, removed from the immediate experience of war and military occupation, who have taken up the task of history.

***

Michiko Ikeda was sixteen-years-old when she left her parents' home in Amagasaki City, Japan, a sprawling suburb just outside Osaka, and headed to Nara in 1948. In Nara she sang the blues to the likes of Futaba Akiko, the famous Japanese songstress of the prewar years. Nara, once the ancient city of the imperial family, was now a bustling military town. While in Nara, Michiko met Louis Olivares, a Mexican American serviceman from Texas. Soon after, they married and had one daughter. In 1954 they left Japan and arrived in the United States where Michiko gave birth to four more daughters. After moving around the US, Louis and Michiko eventually settled in the Highland Park neighborhood of East Los Angeles. Michiko was my maternal grandmother and Louis, my grandfather. This project is both an analysis of those like them—of their generation—and an homage to the legacy they left. As Naoko Shibusawa poignantly recalls, "all historians . . . are looking for their past."[13] My search for history began in 2009 when I was as an undergraduate student at the University of California, Berkeley writing a family immigration history. As I dove deeper into the archive, the literature, and my own memories, I realized that my family's story was extraordinary and common at the same time.

Yet, this history is not mine only. Nor did it begin when my grandparents met, married, or entered the US. The story of the Japanese in America—specifically of Japanese women in America—stretches back to the thousands of Japanese women who immigrated to the US to join their husbands in the early decades of the twentieth century. By expanding the chronological scope of analysis to include both pre- and postwar flows of migration, *Picture Bride, War Bride* asserts that longterm historical studies are essential to understanding the multiple pasts that make up our present.[14] In doing so, this project contributes to scholarship concerned with offering new ways of thinking about the Japanese in America.

Using gender as category of analysis of Japanese immigration and settlement in the United States reveals that amidst racial exclusion, pockets of inclusion allowed women to enter. Indeed, since World War II women immigrants entering the US have outnumbered men, and yet much of the current discussion on immigration neglects this historical shift.[15] This project aims to challenge narratives of the Japanese in America that focus on men and on the Japanese nuclear family by incorporating the stories of the women who married across the color line after World War II. By examining such pockets of inclusion that gender produced, this project demonstrates the importance of examining small windows of inclusion in an otherwise history of exclusion. As Catherine Lee has exclaimed, understanding how, why, and under what circumstance some immigrants have been allowed to immigrate to the US is equally important to understanding why other groups were excluded.[16] There is as much to learn in inclusion as there is to learn in exclusion. For the Japanese in America, heterosexual marriage shaped the paradigms of inclusion and exclusion throughout the twentieth century.

ACKNOWLEDGMENTS

The idea for this book came to me in an undergraduate course. While I was a student at the University of California, Berkeley, I enrolled in S. Deborah Kang's US history course on immigration. For the final project I opted to research and write about my maternal grandmother who had immigrated from Japan to the United States in the early 1950s. I sat in Professor Kang's office one day sharing my grandmother's story when she replied, "Your grandmother was a Japanese war bride." I had never heard this term and was instantly taken by the notion that my grandmother was one of many women who made the trek across the Pacific in the aftermath of World War II as the wives of American servicemen. That was sometime in the spring of 2009, and not a day has gone by since that I don't think of my grandmother and the many women like her.

I must begin by first acknowledging those at Berkeley who nurtured my curiosity and held me up when I was feeling out of place as an almost thirty-year-old undergraduate. Endless thanks to S. Deborah Kang, Waldo E. Martin, Leah Carroll, and the community I found at the Haas and McNair Scholars Programs, as well as the Transfer Re-entry Student Transfer Center (TRSP). A big thank you to my fellow mama bears. While studying at the University of Chicago, I was fortunate enough to be trained by meticulous scholars who I am indebted to for making me the historian I am today. Thank you, Matthew M. Briones, Susan L. Burns, and James T. Sparrow. I am also indebted to the community of courageous thinkers I found at the Center for the Study of Race, Politics, and Culture (CSRPC) and the Center for the Study of Gender and Sexuality (CSGS). Additionally, I thank the Center for East Asian Studies for their support.

I received a predoctoral fellowship from the School of Humanities, Arts, and Social Sciences (SHASS) at the Massachusetts Institute of Technology, which gave me the time and space to complete my graduate work; thank you. I extend my sincerest gratitude to Emma J. Teng, Jeffrey S. Ravel, and Augustín Rayo. I was also fortunate enough to receive a Postdoctoral Fellowship at the Mahindra Humanities Center at Harvard University where I was a part of a wonderful community of scholars, administrators, and staff.

Of course, this work would not be possible without the support of archivists. I would like to thank the many archivists and staff members at the National Archives Records and Administration in San Bruno, CA and College Park, MD who helped me in various ways over the years. I am especially indebted to Karen Kanemoto and Ryan Yokota of the Japanese American Service Committee in Chicago, IL.

I have much love for the many friends who kept me grounded while writing this book. Thank you for your friendship, Marco A. Flores, Jennifer Wang, Veronica Miranda, Irene Lopez, and Sally Sowter. Noriko Yamaguchi, thank you for your astute translations that helped me to bring to life the inner lives of the men I write about in chapter two. Thank you DAB 4 for your friendship at the University of Chicago. I'll never forget the good times we carved out at the "place where fun comes to die." Thank you to Celina Chatman-Nelson for being a breath of fresh air.

Before arriving at Santa Clara University, I spent time on the "alt-ac" track and made several valuable friendships. Thank you to the good folks I met on this part of my journey. At Santa Clara University, I'd like to thank my colleagues in the Department of History who have provided a warm and supportive environment in which I finished this book. A special thank you goes to Nancy Unger who took the time to read the manuscript in its entirety and offered valuable feedback. Thank you to my colleagues at Santa Clara who have helped me navigate the university as a junior faculty member. Santa Clara wouldn't be the same without you all and the community we continue to build. Thank you to the San Jose crew with whom I can "get stupid" free of judgement.

Finally, I want to thank my family. To my mother, Linda Olivares, who has been a source of unwavering strength and inspiration my entire life. Thank you for teaching me how to be a fighter and for always being in my corner. Thank you to the man who helped raised me, Richard Atilano. Although we don't talk these days, I am grateful for the encouragement you offered me as a child and rambunctious teenager. To Marlon

Gomez, my "sweet prince of the ghetto," who has been a real one since day one, your support—emotional and financial—and constant good cheer has helped me to realize my dreams, and I am forever grateful for that, *mil gracias*. Angelina, Elijah, and Emile. You three are my greatest accomplishment. Thank you for always keeping me grounded and bringing joy and meaning to my life. I hope you are proud of the work I have done. To Amir, I hope one day when you read this book you will know your great-great grandmother, Michiko.

NOTES

INTRODUCTION

1 Drawing on the work of Sidney Xu Lu, I use the term "settler migrant" to refer to the first Japanese migrants to arrive in the United States. This framing acknowledges the migration of Japanese nationals alongside the expansion of the Japanese empire. Japanese settler colonialism in Asia and the Americas was encouraged by what Lu refers to as "Malthusian expansionism." See: Lu, Sidney Xu, *The Making of Japanese Settler Colonialism: Malthusianism and Trans-Pacific Migration, 1868–1961* (Cambridge: Cambridge University Press, 2019).

2 Committee on Energy and Natural Resources, Gold Hill Wakamatsu Preservation Act, S. Rep. No. 111–308 (2010); Baur, John E. "California Crops That Failed," *California Historical Society Quarterly* 45, no. 1 (1966): 41–68.

3 *Wakamatsu Colony Centennial, 1869–1969*, stack 2, 7b, box 1, folder 5, Ross Harano Papers and Photograph Collection, Japanese American Service Committee. For more on the Wakamatsu colonists see John E. Van Sant, *Pacific Pioneers: Japanese Journeys to America and Hawaii, 1850–1880* (Urbana: University of Illinois Press, 2000), 122–130.

4 At the Wakamatsu Tea and Silk Colony Festival held in May 2012 to support the preservation of the land, Rep. Doris Matsui (D-CA), a third generation Japanese American (Sansei) stated, "To many Japanese Americans, the Wakamatsu Colony is as symbolic as Plymouth Rock was for the first American colonists. The Gold Hill Wakamatsu Collaborative now has the historic opportunity to acquire this land and preserve the legacy of these early Japanese Americans." *The Rafu Shimpo*, May 8, 2012.

5 Henry Schnell's wife, Jou Schnell, was a Japanese woman from Aizuwakamatsu, Japan. Their marriage also contributed to the interracial makeup of early Japanese America. See John E. Van Sant, *Pacific Pioneers: Japanese Journeys to America and Hawaii, 1850–80* (Urbana: University of Illinois Press, 2000) 125.

6 Cecilia Rasmussen, "Hilltop Grave May Become a Shrine," *Los Angeles Times*, June 10, 2007.

7 Yuji Ichioka, *The Issei: The World of the First Generation Japanese Immigrants, 1885–1924* (New York: The Free Press, 1988), 164.

8 Greg Robinson, *The Great Unknown: Japanese American Sketches* (Boulder: University Press of Colorado, 2016), 4; Yuji Ichioka, "Amerika Nadeshiko: Japanese Immigrant Women in the United States, 1900–1924" *Pacific Historical Review* 49, no. 2 (1980).

9 I use the term "war brides" to refer to the Japanese women who migrated to the United States with American husbands between World War II and the McCarran-Walter Act of 1952. I recognize that this term is imperfect; however, because "war brides" has been used to refer to this pattern of migration in scholarship and popular culture I remain committed to using it for consistency. Other scholars use the term "military brides" to refer to the migration of Asian wives of American servicemen. For example, see Ji-Yeon Yuh, *Beyond the Shadow of Camptown: Korean Military Brides in America* (New York: New York University Press, 2002), 3.

10 Pierrette Hondagneu-Sotelo, *Gendered Transitions: Mexican Experiences of Immigration* (Berkeley: University of California Press, 1994), 2.

11 Baumann, Martin. "Diaspora: Genealogies of Semantics and Transcultural Comparison." *Numen* 47, no. 3 (2000): 328.

12 Moreover, the lack of a gendered analysis of early Japanese immigration assumes that men are without gender. See Yen Le Espiritu, *Asian American Women and Men* (Thousand Oaks, CA: Sage Publications, 1997), 16.

13 For scholarship that uses gender and race as a category of analysis in Japanese immigration, see Evelyn Nakano Glenn, *Unequal Freedom: How Race and Gender Shaped American Citizenship and Labor* (Cambridge, MA: Harvard University Press, 2002); *Issei, Nisei, Warbride: Three Generations of Japanese American Women in Domestic Service* (Philadelphia: Temple University Press, 1986); Paul Spickard, *Mixed Blood: Intermarriage and Ethnic Identity in 20th-Century America* (Madison: University of Wisconsin Press, 1989).

14 Catherine Lee, "'Where the Danger Lies': Race, Gender, and Chinese and Japanese Exclusion in the United States, 1870–1924," *Sociological Forum* 25, no. 2 (2010): 251.

15 Lee, "Where the Danger Lies," 251.

16 Eiichiro Azuma, *Between Two Empires: Race, History, and Transnationalism in Japanese America* (Oxford: Oxford University Press, 2005), 53.

17 Nancy Cott, *Public Vows: A History of Marriage and the Nation* (Cambridge, MA: Harvard University Press, 2000), 4.

18 Peggy Pascoe, *What Comes Naturally: Miscegenation Law and the Making of Race in America* (New York: Oxford University Press, 2009), 2.

19 Pascoe, 2.

20 While marriage legitimized Mitsuko's status in the US, it did not protect her from deportation in the future. "GI and Japanese Wife Arrive to See his Parents," *Chicago Daily Tribune*, Nov 20, 1951.

21 Yen Le Espiritu, *Homebound: Filipino American Lives Across Cultures, Communities, and Countries* (Berkeley: University of California Press, 2003), 47.

22 While male names ending in "ichi" typically signify that they are the first son, Kenichi Sakoda was described by his son, James, as arriving to the US with his older brother, indicating he was not the eldest son. James M. Sakoda, interview by Arthur A. Hansen, August 9–10, 1988, California State University, Fullerton Oral History Program, Japanese American Project.

23 Masao Suzuki, "Success Story? Japanese Immigrant Economic Achievement and Return Migration, 1920–1930," *The Journal of Economic History* 55, no. 4 (2009): 892.

24 Sandra Geiger, *Subverting Exclusion: Transpacific Encounters with Race, Caste, and Borders, 1885–1928* (New Haven, CT: Yale University Press, 2011), 29 and 213.

1. A PARADOX OF EXCLUSION

1 Records of the Immigration and Naturalization Service, San Francisco District, "Immigration Arrival Investigation Files, 1884–1944," file 10443/11–10, box 480, RG 085, National Archives Records and Administration, San Bruno, CA.

2 Jennifer Gee, "Housewives, Men's Villages, and Sexual Respectability: Gender and the Interrogation of Asian Women at the Angel Island Immigration Station," in *Asian/Pacific Islander American Women*, eds. Shirley Hune and Gail M. Nomura (New York: New York University Press, 2003), 90.

3 Eiichiro Azuma, *Between Two Empires: Race, History, and Transnationalism in Japanese America* (New York: Oxford University Press, 2005); Evelyn Nakano Glenn, *Issei, Nisei, War Bride: Three Generations of Japanese American Women in Domestic Service* (Philadelphia: Temple University Press, 1986); Yuji Ichioka, *The Issei: The World of the First Generation Japanese Immigrants, 1885–1924* (New York: Free Press, 1988); Mae Ngai, *Impossible Subjects: Illegal Aliens and the Making of Modern America* (Princeton: Princeton University Press, 2004).

4 Roger Daniels, *The Politics of Prejudice: The Anti-Japanese Movement in California and the Struggle for Japanese Exclusion*, second edition. (Berkeley: University of California Press, 1977), 44.

5 Catherine Lee, *Fictive Kinship: Family Reunification and the Meaning of Race and Nation in American Migration* (New York: Russell Sage Foundation, 2013), 59.

6 Nira Yuval-Davis, "Gender and Nation," *Ethnic and Racial Studies* 16, no. 4 (October 1993): 627.

7 I am indebted to Ashley J. Finigan for introducing me to the term "gender panic." For more see Gilbert Herdt, ed., *Moral Panics, Sex Panics: Fear and the Fight Over Sexual Rights* (New York: New York University Press, 2009); Catherine Lee, "'Where the Danger Lies': Race, Gender, and Chinese and Japanese Exclusion in the United States, 1870–1924," *Sociological Forum* 25, no. 2 (2010).

8 For example, Ronald Takaki describes the family provisions outlined in the Gentlemen's Agreement as a loophole *in Strangers from a Different Shore: A History of Asian Americans* (New York: Back Bay Books, 1998), 46 and 204.

9 Lee, *Fictive Kinship*, 6.

10 Lee, *Fictive Kinship*, 51.

11 Quote taken from the congressional record on April 14, 1924, wherein state senators debated the question of retaining the Gentlemen's Agreement with Japan, though the migration of picture brides had drastically slowed in 1921. Papers relating to the *Foreign Relations of the United States*, 1924, Vol. 2, 378, Office of the Historian, US Department of State.

12 In contrast to the Gentlemen's Agreement, the Page Law of 1875 restricted the migration of women for "immoral purposes" which many scholars have shown was a euphemism for all Chinese women migrants regardless of occupation. Thus, Chinese migrants were not afforded the same accommodations as the Japanese which resulted in large numbers of Chinese bachelor communities. For more on the privileges of marriage see Nancy F. Cott, *Public Vows: A History of Marriage and the Nation* (Cambridge, MA: Harvard University Press, 2000). For more on the politics of the Gentlemen's Agreement and its influence on the Dillingham Commission see Katherine Benton-Cohen, *Inventing the Immigration Problem: The Dillingham Commission and Its Legacy* (Cambridge, MA: Harvard University Press, 2018), chapter 2, especially page 55.

13 The Naturalization Act of 1790 restricted naturalized citizenship to "free white" persons. The Naturalization Act was amended in 1870 to include persons of African descent. In 1922, *Ozawa v. United States* ruled that the Japanese were not free whites and thus ineligible for naturalization.

14 Brenda Frink, "San Francisco Pioneer Mother Monument: Maternalism, Racial Order, and the Politics of Memorialization, 1907–1915," *American Quarterly* 64, no. 1, 90.

15 The exception of "parents, wives, and children of Japanese residents in America," was first introduced by the Japanese in December 1907, in response to proposition 2 of the agreement. Proposition 2 called for Japan to deny passports to "skilled or unskilled" laborers and "all those who from choice or from force of circumstances are likely to become laborers if they enter the United States." The modification of proposition 2 was accepted by US Secretary of State Elihu Root and telegrammed to Thomas O'Brien, U.S. Ambassador at Tokyo, on January 23, 1908. See: "Memorandum by the Division of Far Eastern Affairs, Department of State" in "Papers relating to the *Foreign Relations of the United States*," 1924, Vol. 2, 339.

16 Eithne Luibhéid. *Entry Denied: Controlling Sexuality at the Border* (Minneapolis: University of Minnesota Press, 2002), 11.

17 In April 1921 the House Committee on Immigration and Naturalization published four volumes of hearings entitled, "Japanese Immigration." In 1,490 pages, the House Committee debated the "Japanese problem." A total of 154 individuals appeared before the committee as witnesses. According to Sydney Gulick, an outspoken supporter of the Japanese in America, the purpose and scope of the hearings were not clearly defined. He lamented, "Apparently the Committee was ready to hear anything and everything which anybody wanted to say about the Japanese." The lack of a clearly defined agenda "left the door wide open for aimless ramblings and wanderings" that were "quite irrelevant." However, these seemingly random ramblings of the committee and the 154 individuals who served as witnesses reveals the varied, contrasting views of the Japanese in the American imagination. Throughout the 1,490 pages, politicians, journalists, community leaders, farmers, businessmen, and other ordinary people debated the problem of Japanese immigration. What is most striking is the way Japanese women's labor

and reproductive power were at the center of much of the conversation. Sidney Lewis Gulick, *Should Congress Enact Special Laws Affecting Japanese?: A Critical Examination of the "Hearings Before the Committee On Immigration and Naturalization," Held in California, July 1920*, The National Committee on American Japanese Relations, New York, 1922, 5–6.

18 *Japanese Immigration: Hearings Before the Committee on Immigration and Naturalization*, H.R. Rep. 66th Cong. 2nd sess., 1920, at 40.

19 John P. Irish, "Articles: Japanese Question" M033, box 13, folder 29, John Powell Irish Papers, Department of Special Collections, Stanford University Libraries, Stanford, CA.

20 Japanese Immigration, 48.

21 Japanese Immigration, 48.

22 Japanese Immigration, 71.

23 "Irish and Mrs. Scott Talk Against Suffrage," San Francisco Examiner, Thursday, October 05, 1911.

24 Roger Daniels, *The Politics of Prejudice: The Anti-Japanese Movement in California and the Struggle for Japanese Exclusion* (Berkeley: University of California Press, 1977), 85.

25 Peggy Pascoe, *What Comes Naturally: Miscegenation Law and the Making of Race in America* (New York: Oxford University Press, 2009), 85–87.

26 Nayan Shah, *Stranger Intimacy: Contesting Race, Sexuality, and the Law in the North American West* (Berkeley: University of California Press, 2011).

27 "Why Brown Men are a Dire Menace," *San Francisco Chronicle*, April 10, 1905; "Japanese A Menace to American Women," *San Francisco Chronicle*, March 1, 1905.

28 Natalia Molina shows how racialized discourse constructed the Japanese as a health threat to white Americans, bolstering claims about their inability to assimilate, and justifying their exclusion from political and social life in Los Angeles. See: Natalia Molina, *Fit to be Citizens: Public Health and Race in Los Angeles, 1879–1939* (Berkeley: University of California Press, 2006).

29 Catherine Lee, "'Where the Danger Lies': Race, Gender, and Chinese and Japanese Exclusion in the United States, 1870–1924," *Sociological Forum* 25, no. 2 (2010): 262.

30 For example, see Roger Daniels, *The Politics of Prejudice: The Anti-Japanese Movement in California and the Struggle for Japanese Exclusion* (Berkeley: University of California Press, 1977); Yuji Ichioka, *The Issei: The World of the First Generation Japanese Immigrants, 1885–1924* (New York: The Free Press, 1988); Eiichiro Azuma, *Between Two Empires: Race, History, and Transnationalism in Japanese America* (Oxford: Oxford University Press, 2005).

31 Martha Gardner, *The Qualities of a Citizen: Women, Immigration, and Citizenship, 1870–1965* (Princeton, NJ: Princeton University Press, 2005), 41.

32 Lu Ann Jones. *Mama Learned Us to Work: Farm Women in the New South* (Chapel Hill: University of North Carolina Press, 2002).

33 Masakatsu Okado, "The Women of Rural Japan: An Overview of the Twentieth Century," in *Farmers and Village Life in Japan*, ed. Ann Waswo and Nishida Yoshiaki (London: Routledge, 2003), 41–43.
34 Ibid.
35 Kelli Y. Nakamura, "Issei Women and Work: Washerwomen, Prostitutes, Midwives, and Barbers," *The Hawaiian Journal of History* 49 (2015): 121.
36 Midge Ayukawa, "Good Wives and Wise Mothers: Japanese Picture Brides in Early Twentieth-Century British Columbia," *BC Studies*, nos. 105–106 (Spring/Summer 1995): 118.
37 Gardner, *The Qualities of a Citizen*, 41; "Governor Asks U.S. Action to Bar Japanese," *San Francisco Chronicle*, June 22, 1920.
38 Yen Le Espiritu, *Asian American Women and Men* (Thousand Oaks, CA: Sage Publications, 1997), 17.
39 "Japanese 'Picture Brides' Become Frights in California," *Literary Digest* 62 (August 9, 1919): 53.
40 "No More babies in 2015," *New York Tribune*, Dec 31, 1910.
41 Myre St. Wald Iseman, *Race Suicide* (New York: The Cosmopolitan Press, 1912), 5.
42 Ibid., 135. For more on women's greater independence in industrializing America and the fear and backlash it caused, see Kathy Peiss, *Cheap Amusements: Working Women and Leisure in Turn-of-the-Century New York* (Philadelphia: Temple University Press, 1986) and Nancy MacLean, "The Leo Frank Case Reconsidered: Gender and Sexual Politics in the Making of Reactionary Populism" *Journal of American History*, 78, no. 3 (1991) pp. 917–948.
43 Phelan's campaign is eerily similar to the 1994 California Proposition 187, the Save our State initiative that sought to bar undocumented immigrants from accessing education, welfare, and healthcare services. Prop. 187 was aimed at women and children as the measure would have directly and most severely affected them. See: Jonathan Xaviar Inda, "Foreign Bodies: Migrants, Parasites, and the Pathological Nation." *Discourse* 22, no. 3 (2000): 46–62.
44 *Japanese Immigration: Hearings before the Committee on Immigration and Naturalization*, 22.
45 Ibid., 209.
46 State Board of Control, California. *California and the Oriental: Japanese, Chinese, and Hindus*, Report of State Board of Control of California to Gov. WM. D. Stephens, June 19, 1920, 37.
47 State Board of Control, 40 and 160.
48 Beth Lew-Williams shows how physical violence—lynching and mass murder—was only one method to exclude the Chinese. See Lew-Williams, Beth, *The Chinese Must Go: Violence, Exclusion, and the Making of the Alien in America* (Cambridge, MA: Harvard University Press, 2018).
49 Evelyn Nakano Glenn, *Issei, Nisei, Warbride: Three Generations of Japanese American Women in Domestic Service* (Philadelphia: Temple University

Press, 1986), 50. Martha Gardner describes the Gentlemen's Agreement as having concluded in 1920, though it seems in practice the Japanese did not stop issuing passports until 1921. See: Martha Gardner, *The Qualities of a Citizen*, 44.

50 Peter Duus, "Presidential Address: Weapons of the Weak, Weapons of the Strong—The Development of the Japanese Political Cartoon." *The Journal of Asian Studies* 60, no. 4 (2001): 965–97.

51 Ichioka, *The Issei*, 28.

52 Yuji Ichioka, "Ameyuki-san: Japanese Prostitutes in Nineteenth-Century America," *Amerasia Journal* 4, no. 1 (1977): 4.

53 Ichioka, *The Issei*, 34.

54 Kelli Y. Nakamura's work demonstrates how Issei women in Hawai'i found opportunities for self-determination in the toilsome world of plantation life. See Kelli Y. Nakamura, "Issei Women and Work: Washerwomen, Prostitutes, Midwives, and Barbers," *The Hawaiian Journal of History*, 49 (2015).

55 Kazuhiro Oharazeki, "Listening to the Voices of 'Other' Women in Japanese North America: Japanese Prostitutes and Barmaids in the American West, 1887–1920," *Journal of American Ethnic History* 32, no. 4 (Summer 2013): 26.

56 Cecilia M. Tsu, "Sex, Lies, and Agriculture: Reconstructing Japanese Immigrant Relations in Rural California, 1900–1913," *Pacific Historical Review* 78, no. 2 (2009): 176.

57 "Immoral Japanese: Two Girls Who Will Be Sent Home," *San Francisco Chronicle*, March 30, 1890; "Immoral Japanese," *San Francisco Chronicle*, April 6, 1893.

58 Immigration Arrival Case Files, RG 085, box 910, folder 14315/23.4, National Archives Records and Administration, San Bruno, CA.

59 Oharazeki, "Listening to the Voices," 17.

60 Judy Yung, *Unbound Feet: A Social History of Chinese Women in San Francisco* (Berkeley: University of California Press, 1995), 73.

61 Dennie Chadbourne, Letter to Donaldina Cameron. Sept. 20, 1915. Immigration Case Files, RG 085, box 910, folder 14315/23.4, National Archives Records and Administration, San Bruno, CA.

62 Immigration Arrival Case Files, RG 085, box 910, folder 14315/23.4, National Archives Records and Administration, San Bruno, CA.

63 According to the 1930 US Census, Nobutaro remarried a woman named Rei Yamahata, who had arrived in the US in 1919. 1930 US Census, Los Angeles County, California, p. 4A, enumeration district 408, image 293.0, FHL microfilm 2339883, roll 148, National Archives, Washington DC.

64 Azuma, *Between Two Empires*, 34.

65 Azuma, *Between Two Empires*, 35.

66 Ichioka, *The Issei*, 179.

67 Kazuhiro Oharazeki, "Anti-prostitution Campaigns in Japan and the American West, 1890–1920: A Transpacific Comparison," *Pacific Historical Review* 82, no. 2 (2013): 176.

68 Oharazeki, "Listening to the Voices," 17.

69 Chrissy Yee Lau, "'Ashamed of Certain Japanese': The Politics of Affect in Japanese Women's Immigration Exclusion, 1919–1924," In *Gendering the Trans-Pacific World: Diaspora, Empire, and Race* eds. Catherine Ceniza Choy and Judy Tzu-Chun Wu (Leiden, The Netherlands: Brill, 2017), 208.

70 "Japanese Women," *Boston Globe Magazine*, Nov. 25, 1917.

71 Ibid.

72 Ikuko Asaka, "'Colored Men of the East': African Americans and the Instability of Race in US-Japan Relations," *American Quarterly* 66, no. 4 (December 2014): 977.

73 Naoko Shibusawa, *America's Geisha Ally: Reimagining the Japanese Enemy* (Cambridge, MA: Harvard University Press, 2006), 22.

74 During the same period, Christopher Reed shows how East Coast views of the Japanese were strikingly different than those on the West Coast. In his analysis of *Japanism* he dedicates an entire chapter on elite Bostonians' interest in Japan, showing how wealthy Bostonian men and some women viewed Japan as a place where elite masculinity thrived. The image of the Japanese woman as "modest," "dutiful," "faithful," and "affectionate" was made concrete by her subordination to the masculine power that ruled her country. In other words, the Madame Butterfly motif fit nicely within wealthy Bostonians' racial thinking about the Japanese, and because the Japanese population in Boston was tiny at the time, fear of the "Yellow Peril" did not take root as it did on the West Coast. See Christopher Reed, *Bachelor Japanists: Japanese Aesthetics and Western Cultures* (New York: Columbia University Press, 2017), fn. 1, 295.

75 Katherine Benton-Cohen, *Inventing the Immigration Problem: The Dillingham Commission and Its Legacy* (Cambridge, MA: Harvard University Press, 2018), 11.

76 Evelyn Nakano Glenn, *Issei, Nisei, Warbride: Three Generations of Japanese American Women in Domestic Service* (Philadelphia: Temple University Press, 1986), 50.

2. ISSEI BACHELORS

1 Case file for Kazuyuki Araki, RG 8, series 3, box 1, folder 22. Japanese American Service Committee Legacy Center, Chicago, IL.

2 While it is not clear from the extant records that Araki was indeed escaping tradition by migrating to Japan, we do know that most Issei men who migrated to the United States were "surplus" sons and were seeking to evade the life accorded to second and third sons in Japan. See: Masakatsu Okado, "The Women of Rural Japan: An Overview of the Twentieth Century," in *Farmers and Village Life in Japan*, ed. Ann Waswo and Nishida Yoshiaki (London: Routledge, 2003), 41–43.

3 Case file for Kazuyuki Araki. RG 8, series 3, box 1, folder 22. Japanese American Service Committee Legacy Center, Chicago, IL.

4 Hondagneu-Sotelo, Pierrette. *Gendered Transitions Mexican Experiences of Immigration* (University of California Press, 1994).
5 Joan Scott, "Gender: A Useful Category of Historical Analysis." *The American Historical Review* 91, no. 5 (1986), 1056.
6 Pierrette Hondagneu-Sotelo, *Gendered Transitions: Mexican Experiences of Immigration* (Berkeley: University of California Press, 1994), 3.
7 Howard Chudacoff, *The Age of the Bachelor: Creating an American Subculture* (Princeton, NJ: Princeton University Press, 1999), 3–5.
8 Michelle Caswell, "Seeing Yourself in History: Community Archives and the Fight Against Symbolic Annihilation," *The Public Historian* 36, no. 4 (2016); George Gerbner and Larry Gross, "Living with Television: The Violence of Profile," *Journal of Communication*, 26, no. 2 (Spring 1976): 182.
9 Michelle Caswell, "Seeing Yourself in History," 26.
10 Deborah Meiko King Burns, "A Brief History of the JASC," The Japanese American Service Committee Legacy Center, Chicago, IL, 1989.
11 Japanese American Service Committee Legacy Center, "About the JASC," Japanese American Service Committee of Chicago, accessed December 3, 2012, https://jasc-chicago.org/about-us/.
12 Eiichiro Azuma, *Between Two Empires: Race, History, and Transnationalism in Japanese America* (Oxford: Oxford University Press, 2005), 38.
13 Azuma, 38.
14 Stephen Fugita and Marilyn Fernandez, *Altered Lives, Enduring Community: Japanese Americans Remember Their World War II Incarceration* (Seattle: University of Washington Press, 2004), 134.
15 Chudacoff, *The Age of the Bachelor*, 4.
16 Robert E. Park, "Human Migration and the Marginal Man," *American Journal of Sociology* 33, no. 6 (May 1928).
17 Emma Jinhua Teng, *Eurasian: Mixed Identities in the United States, China, and Hong Kong, 1842–1943* (Berkeley: University of California Press, 2013), 143.
18 Park, "Human Migration," 888.
19 Case file for Hideki Fukuzawa. RG 8, series 3, box 1, folder 22. Japanese American Service Committee Legacy Center, Chicago, IL.
20 The "Alien Crew List" contains a column titled "Evidence of Intention to Remain in the US." Each crew member's name, reads "no" including Fukuzawa, line 6. "Crew Lists of Vessels Arriving at Seattle, Washington, 1903–1917." RG 085, M1399, 15 rolls. National Archives, Washington, DC.
21 US Selective Service System, "World War I Selective System Draft Registration Cards, 1917–1918." RG 4, M1509, 582 rolls. National Archives and Records Administration, Washington, DC.
22 1930 US Census, Los Angeles County, California, p. 4A, enumeration district 408, image 293.0, FHL microfilm 2339883, roll 148, National Archives, Washington DC;1940 US Census, Los Angeles County, California, p. 3B, enumeration district 60–736, roll T627–378, National Archives, Washington DC.

23 Records About Japanese Americans Relocated During World War II, created, 1988–1989, documenting the period 1942–1946, Department of Justice, Civil Rights Division, Records of the War Relocation Authority, RG 210, Japanese-American Internee Data File, 1942–1946, National Archives, College Park, MD.

24 Also known as the Dillingham Commission, named after its chairman, the Republican Senator, William Dillingham. The figures above were, in reality, much larger. The numbers listed are from those individuals who reported complete data. In addition, the commission reported that the number of Japanese working on the railroads was "considerably larger than the figures would indicate, however, for three or four railroad companies are employing them in considerable numbers." Another estimate found that the 3,843 Japanese rail hands reported by company managers was too small since the statistics were taken in the off months, when many Japanese had abandoned the railroad for the fields. It is important to note, that "Asiatics" was often a euphemism to mean the Japanese during this period. US Immigration Commission, Immigrants in Industries, Part 23–25: Japanese and Other Immigrant races in the Pacific Coast and Rocky Mountain States (Washington D.C., 1911), 8, 11.

25 The commission was made up of a bipartisan committee formed under pressure from Nativist anti-immigrant groups to restrict the flow of labor migration into the United States. The report bolstered support for the passage of the National Quota Act of 1924, which thereby restricted the immigration of all nonwhite people signaling the beginning of the era of exclusion in American immigration history.

26 *Wakamatsu Colony Centennial, 1869–1969*, stack 2, 7b, box 1, folder 5, Ross Harano Papers and Photograph Collection, Japanese American Service Committee, Chicago, IL.

27 Geiger, *Subverting Exclusion*, 16–17; George De Vos and Wagatsuma Hiroshi, *Japan's Invisible Race: Caste in Culture and Personality* (Berkeley: University of California Press, 1967), 10–20.

28 Geiger, 44.

29 Yamato Ichihashi, *Japanese in the United States* (Stanford, CA: Stanford University Press, 1932), 82.

30 Geiger, *Subverting Exclusion*, 44.

31 Geiger, *Subverting Exclusion*, 45.

32 In a 1924 Survey of Race Relations directed by Robert E. Park, it was noted that Florin, CA was home to the less desirable Japanese who possessed an "unsavory reputation," opposite of Japanese living in Livingston who were said to be the ideal Japanese because they were "Americanized" Christians who did not compete with the white man. See: Survey of Race Relations records, box 1, office file, 1914–1927, Hoover Institution Archives; interview with Mrs. C.S. Machida. Box No.25. Fol. 73; Emma Fong Kuno, "My Oriental Husbands." Survey of Race Relations records. Box no. 25. Fol. 53.

33 Hiroshi Ito, "*Japan's Outcastes in the United States*," in George De Vos and Wagatsuma Hiroshi, *Japan's Invisible Race: Caste in Culture and Personality* (Berkeley: University of California Press, 1967), 200–221.
34 George De Vos and Hiroshi Wagatsuma, *Japan's Invisible Race: Caste in Culture and Personality*, 113.
35 DeVos and Hiroshi, 116.
36 Sandra Geiger, *Subverting Exclusion*, 15.
37 1930 US Census, Los Angeles County, California, National Archives, Washington DC.
38 Mae M. Ngai, *Impossible Subjects: Illegal Aliens and the Making of Modern America* (Princeton, NJ: Princeton University Press, 2004), 104.
39 Case file for Kenji Nakemoto, RG 8, series 3, box 1, folder 5, Japanese American Service Committee Legacy Center, Chicago, IL. For Japanese and Filipino labor relations see: Matthew M. Briones, *Jim and Jap Crow: A Cultural History of the 1940s Interracial America* (Princeton, NJ: Princeton University Press, 2012), 39.
40 Ngai, *Impossible Subjects*, 27.
41 In 1922, *Takao Ozawa v. United States* ruled that the Japanese were not white and therefore barred from naturalization.
42 Japanese citizens also entered the US at the US-Mexico border. See Eiichiro Azuma, "Japanese Immigrant Settler Colonialism in the U.S.-Mexico Borderlands and the U.S. Racial-Imperialist Politics of the Hemispheric "Yellow Peril." *Pacific Historical Review*, 83, no. 2 (2014): 263.
43 Ngai, 49.
44 Tina Takemoto, "Looking for Jiro Onuma: A Queer Meditation on the Incarceration of Japanese Americans during World War II." *GLQ: A Journal of Lesbian And Gay Studies* 20, no. 3 (2014).
45 Takemoto, 241.
46 Historian, Amy Sueyoshi has detailed Noguchi's rise in America's literary circles alongside his quest for romantic fulfillment during a time of "extreme sexual depravation and discrimination for Asians." See: Amy Haruko Sueyoshi, *Queer Compulsions: Race, Nation, and Sexuality in the Affairs of Yone Noguchi* (Honolulu: University of Hawai'i Press, 2012).
47 Amy Lowe Meger, "Historic Resource Study: Minidoka Internment National Monument," National Park Service, US Department of the Interior. Seattle, WA, 2005, 1.
48 Bannister, Robert C. "Dorothy Swain Thomas: Soziologischer Objectivismus: Der Harte Weg in die Profession." In *Frauen in der Soziologie: Neun Portrats*, ed. Claudia Honegger und Teresa Wobbe. Munich: C.H. Beck, 1998.
49 Briones, 114.
50 James M. Sakoda, interview by Arthur A. Hansen, August 9–10, 1988, California State University, Fullerton Oral History Program, Japanese American Project, 392.

51 The War Relocation Authority first administered the "Application for Leave Clearance," infamously known as the "loyalty questionnaire," in early 1943. The questionnaire "required all adult internees to fill out a lengthy registration form to ascertain their loyalty to the United States." The questionnaire had two immediate objectives: it was used to assess the loyalty of potential volunteer combatants as well as those willing and qualified to resettle in the Midwest or East Coast, away from the western Pacific. Second, the questionnaire was created to "promote Japanese American's citizenship and assimilation." (Ngai, *Impossible Subjects*, 181 and 182)

52 James M. Sakoda, "Reminiscences of a Participant Observer," in *Views from Within: The Japanese American Evacuation and Resettlement Study*, ed. Yuji Ichioka. (Los Angeles, CA: Asian American Studies Center, University of California, Los Angeles, 1989), 393.

53 Ibid.

54 Ngai, *Impossible Subjects*, 200.

55 Sakoda, "Reminiscences, 228–229.

56 Dorothy Swaine Thomas, *The Salvage* (Berkeley: University of California Press, 1952), 469.

57 John Howard, *Concentration Camps on the Home Front: Japanese Americans in the House of Jim Crow* (Chicago, IL: University of Chicago Press, 2008), 115.

58 Tina Takemoto, "Looking for Jiro Onuma," 261; John Howard, *Concentration Camps on the Home Front: Japanese Americans in the House of Jim Crow* (Chicago, IL: University of Chicago Press, 2008), 113–123.

59 Yuji Ichioka, ed., *Views From Within: The Japanese American Evacuation and Resettlement Study* (Los Angeles: University of California Press, 1989), 249.

60 Hisaye Yamamoto, "Las Vegas Charley," in *Seventeen Syllables* (New Brunswick, NJ: Rutgers University Press), 80. For more on the ways incarceration affected families, women, and gender relations, see Matsumoto, Valerie. "Japanese American Women during World War II," in *Major Problems in American Women's History* (Houghton Miffin, 2007) 388–408.

61 United States War Liquidation Agency, "People in Motion: The Postwar Adjustment of Evacuated Japanese Americans," United States Department of the Interior (1947), 168.

62 Letter from Nobuko Daiko to Matsuhiro Daiko, translated by Noriko Yamaguchi. Case file for Matsuhiro Daiko, RG 8, series 3, box 1, folder 38, Japanese American Service Committee Legacy Center, Chicago, IL.

63 Olesky, Walter. "A New Way of Life for Elderly Japanese-Americans." *Chicago Tribune*, August 8, 1965.

64 Case file for Kenji Nakemoto, RG 8, series 3, box 1, folder 5, Japanese American Service Committee Legacy Center, Chicago, IL.

65 Letter from Yukie Nakamoto to Kenji Nakamoto, translated by Noriko Yamaguchi. Case file Kenji Nakemoto, RG 8, series 3, box 1, folder 50, Japanese American Service Committee Legacy Center, Chicago, IL.

66 Letter from Hideki "Hugo" Fukuzawa to JASC, translated by Noriko Yamaguchi. Case file for Hideki "Hugo" Fukuzawa, RG 8, series 3, box 1, folder 52, Japanese American Service Committee Legacy Center, Chicago, IL.

67 Case file for Hideki "Hugo" Fukuzawa, RG 8, series 3, box 1, folder 52, Japanese American Service Committee Legacy Center, Chicago, IL.

3. THE US OCCUPATION OF JAPAN AND THE MAKING OF POSTWAR JAPANESE AMERICA

1 Setsuko Williams (Pseudonym used), interviewed by author, Marin City, CA, July 7, 2010. I confirmed details from Setsuko's interview whenever possible. For example, she stated that she arrived in the United States in 1951, but the Immigration Passenger and Crew List shows that she arrived on January 3, 1952 to the Port of Seattle, Washington aboard the USS *General E.T. Collins*. Small discrepancies are anticipated when interviewing a person of advanced age; however, Setsuko demonstrated much physical and mental vigor. Her account is otherwise deemed true and viable.

2 During the Allied Occupation of Japan from 1945 to 1952, American men and Japanese women worked with one another. After World War II, Japan was left in dire conditions. Its political, economic, and social structures were left in ruins. The US military presence provided some economic stability to Japan's war-torn citizens. Its bases and the immediate surrounding area became the economic livelihood for locals. Young Japanese women in search of work flocked to the cities where the American military was present. These women, from varying educational and socioeconomic backgrounds, sought work with the American military in Japan in order to support their families. For many of the young women, it was the first time they had worked outside the home. See Elfrieda Shukert and Barbara Scibetta, *War Brides of World War II* (Novato, CA: Presidio Press, 1988), 187.

3 "GI Fraternization Allowed in Japan," *New York Times*, July 12, 1946; "Chaplains' Aid Asked to End Fraternizing," *New York Times*, April 3, 1946.

4 John Dower, *Embracing Defeat: Japan in the Wake of World War II* (New York: W.W. Norton & Company, 1999), 40; Takemae Eiji, *Inside the GHQ: The Allied Occupation of Japan and Its Legacy* (New York: Continuum, 2002), 57.

5 Some argue that the US Occupation of Japan still exists today, primarily on the island of Okinawa. In her work on prostitution during the Allied Occupation, Sarah Kovner argues that the occupation of Japan should be considered within the broader concept of the term "occupation" and the condition of compromised sovereignty resulting from a foreign military presence. According to Kovner, the Allied Occupation of Japan, which officially began in 1945 and ended in 1952, "may be said to have lasted in Japan through the Korean War years and continuing on until 1972, when Okinawa reverted to Japanese control." See Sarah Kovner, *Occupied Power: Sex Workers and Servicemen in Postwar Japan* (Stanford, CA: Stanford University Press, 2012), 5.

6 Kovner, 56.

7 Dower, *Embracing Defeat*, 134.
8 Stephen Murphy Shigematsu's Japanese mother and American GI father met while working at the US General Headquarters. See Shigematsu, *When Half Is Whole: Multiethnic Asian American Identities* (Stanford, CA: Stanford University Press, 2012), 7.
9 Beth Bailey and David Farber, *The First Strange Place: Race and Sex in World War II Hawaii* (Baltimore, MD: John Hopkins University Press, 1992), 17.
10 Peggy Pascoe, *What Comes Naturally: Miscegenation Law and the Making of Race in America* (Oxford: Oxford University Press, 2009), 205–284; Philip E. Wolgin and Irene Bloemraad, "'Our Gratitude to Our Soldiers': Military Spouses, Family Re-Unification, and Postwar Immigration Reform." *The Journal of Interdisciplinary History* 41, no. 1 (2010): 27–60.
11 Mae M. Ngai, *Impossible Subjects: Illegal Aliens and the Making of Modern America* (Princeton, NJ: Princeton University Press, 2004), 27.
12 Public Law 271, 79th Congress, 1st session, page 659, December 28, 1945.
13 Sandra Zeiger, *Entangling Alliances: Foreign War Brides and American Soldiers in the Twentieth Century* (New York: New York University Press, 2010), 181.
14 Martha Gardner, *The Qualities of a Citizen: Women, Immigration, and Citizenship, 1870–1965* (Princeton, NJ: Princeton University Press, 2009), 15.
15 Philip E. Wolgin, and Irene Bloemraad, "Our Gratitude," 37.
16 Alex Lubin, *Romance and Rights: The Politics of Interracial Intimacy, 1945–1954* (Jackson: University of Mississippi Press, 2005) 97.
17 Lubin, 67.
18 Gerald Horne, *Facing the Rising Sun: African Americans, Japan, and the Rise of Afro-Asian Solidarity* (New York: New York University Press, 2018), 151.
19 For more on Japanese articulations of Afro-Asian relations, see Yuichiro Onishi, *Transpacific Antiracism: Afro-Asian Solidarity in 20th-Century Black America, Japan, and Okinawa* (New York: New York University Press, 2013), especially chapter three.
20 In fact, Horne explains that Afro-Asian bonds did not perish in the aftermath of World War II, as some scholars have argued, but instead were suggested in the "peculiar intimacies" between Black men and Japanese women. See Horne, *Facing the Rising Sun*, 163.
21 My analysis of the politics of desire in Occupied Japan builds upon the work of Vanita Reddy and Anantha Sudhakar who encourage scholars working in Afro-Asian studies to disinvest in analysis of synchronic time, for it privileges "cross-racial alliances that occur contemporaneously." Instead, the authors urge a "different logic of temporality" in what they name a "politics of deferral" wherein connections to a shared struggle become knowable only afterwards and through queer and feminist analysis. See: Vanita Reddy and Anantha Sudhakar, "Introduction: Feminist and Queer Afro-Asian Formations," in *The Scholar and Feminist* 14, no. 3, 2018.

22 Katherine Davenport to Clifford R. Moore, 1950, RG II, box A650, folder "US Army, Base Discrimination," NAACP Papers, Library of Congress, Washingon, DC.
23 "Group may Sue to Open Park." *Baltimore Afro-American*, Aug 19, 1950.
24 Jeff Wiltse, *Contested Waters: A Social History of Swimming Pools in America* (Chapel Hill: The University of North Carolina Press, 2007).
25 Davenport to Moore, NAACP papers, Library of Congress.
26 For more on Black Orientalism during the occupation, see Yasuhiro Okada. "'Cold War Black Orientalism": Race, Gender, and African American Representations of Japanese Women during the Early 1950s." *Journal of American & Canadian Studies*, no. 27 (March 2009).
27 Cathy D. Knepper, *Jersey Justice: The Story of the Trenton Six* (New Brunswick, New Jersey: Rivergate Books, 2011), 85.
28 "Trenton Man Named U.S. Officer," *Baltimore Afro-American*, October 4, 1952.
29 Roy Wilkins to Frank Pace Jr., 1950, RG II, box A650, folder "US Army, Base Discrimination," NAACP Papers, Library of Congress, Washington, DC.
30 Frank Pace Jr. to Roy Wilkins, 1950, RG II, box A650, folder "US Army, Base Discrimination," NAACP Papers, Library of Congress, Washington, DC.
31 "Reader Tells of Race Violence in Japan," *The Chicago Defender*, July 6, 1946.
32 Theodore Gilmore Bilbo, *Take Your Choice: Separation or Mongrelization* (Poplarville, Miss.: Dream House Pub. Co., 1947).
33 See also Yukiko Koshiro. *Transpacific Racisms and the US Occupation of Japan* (New York: Columbia University Press, 1999), 56; J.M. Throckmorton. "What The People Think: GI Reports Japan Doesn't Know Jim Crow," *The Pittsburgh Courier*, Feb 26, 1949.
34 Mary Louise Roberts. *What Soldiers Do: Sex and the American GI in World War II France* (Chicago: University of Chicago Press, 2013), 233.
35 "Court Martial Trials," *The Chicago Defender*, Oct 14, 1944; Roberts, *What Soldiers Do*, 236–238.
36 "Forum Fact and Opinion," *The Pittsburgh Courier*, Mar 13, 1937.
37 "Forum: Fact and Opinion. "*The Pittsburgh Courier*, Mar. 13, 1937.
38 Reginald Kearney, "The Pro-Japanese Utterances of W.E.B. Du Bois," *Contributions in Black Studies* 13 (1995): 209.
39 For more on pro-Japanese thinking among Black Americans see: Gerald Horne, "Tokyo Bound: African Americans and Japan Confront White Supremacy" in "Blacks and Asians: Revisiting Racial Formations," *Souls: A Critical Journal in Black Politics, Culture, and Society* 3, no. 3 (Summer 2001); Marc S. Gallicchio, *The African American Encounter with Japan and China Black Internationalism in Asia, 1895–1945* (Chapel Hill: University of North Carolina Press, 2000); Reginald Kearney, "The Pro-Japanese Utterances of W.E.B. Du Bois," *Contributions in Black Studies* 13, Article 7; Yuichiro Onishi, *Transpacific Antiracism: Afro-Asian Solidarity in Twentieth-century Black America, Japan, and Okinawa* (New York: New York University Press, 2013).

40 Gerald Horne, *Race War: White Supremacy and the Japanese Attack on the British Empire* (New York: New York University Press, 2004).
41 Horne, *Race War*, 109–113; Kearney, "The Pro-Japanese Utterances of W.E.B. Du Bois," 203.
42 Afro-Asian intimacies in Occupied Japan existed beyond heterosexual encounters; this article offers but one view. Still to be explored are the encounters between Black women and the Japanese as well as the homosocial bonds between Black GIs and Japanese men (mostly family members of Japanese wives and girlfriends) among others. Moreover, I recognize that women's experiences are marginalized within the broader field of Afro-Asian studies. For more on new directions in Afro-Asian studies see Vanita Reddy and Anantha Sudhakar, "Introduction: Feminist and Queer Afro-Asian Formations," in *The Scholar and Feminist* 14.3, 2018.
43 William T. Bowers, William M. Hammond, and George L. MacGarrigle, *Black Soldier, White Army: The 24th Infantry Regiment in Korea, Center for Military History*, Washington, DC, 1996, 42.
44 Maurice A. Butler, *Out from the Shadow: The Story of Charles L. Glittens Who Broke the Color Barrier in the United States Secret Service* (Washington DC: Xlibris Publishing, 2012), 23.
45 Bowers et al., *Black Soldier*, 48.
46 "Americans Make Themselves at Home in Japan," *Baltimore Afro-American*, April 17, 1948.
47 Despite the positive assessment of the Japanese, Duckett and other Black journalists thought little of using the racial slur—Japs—to refer to the Japanese people as this was a commonly used word in the US. Alfred A. Duckett, "Japs Teach Americans Democracy, GI Reports," *Baltimore Afro-American*, April 22, 1950.
48 Sidney Jordan, "Dancing at Zanzibar" interviewed by Kathryn Tolbert for *Japanese War Brides: An Oral History*. Accessed May 6, 2018, http://www.warbrideproject.com/chance-meetings-in-japan/dancing-at-the-zanzibar/.
49 Yasuhiro Okada, "Negotiating Race and Womanhood Across the Pacific: African American Women in Japan under U.S. Military Occupation, 1945–1952." *Black Women, Gender, and Families* 6, no. 1 (Spring 2012): 72.
50 Bok-Lim C. Kim, "Asian Wives of U.S. Servicemen: Women in Shadows," *Amerasia Journal* 4 no. 1 (1977): 99.
51 Duckett, "Japs Teach Americans."
52 Eiji Takamae, *Inside the GHQ: The Allied Occupation of Japan and its Legacy* (New York: Continuum, 2002), 131.
53 Lee Hildegard, "A 'Child of Jazz' Bridges Fillmore and Japantown," *San Francisco Chronicle*, September 10, 2008.
54 "3-Year Courtship in Japan: Baltimore GI, Tokyo Bride, Find Love Is All Languages," *Baltimore Afro-American*, April 26, 1952.
55 Takemae Eiji, *Inside the GHQ*, 131.
56 Duckett, "Japs Teach Americans."

57 Alex Lubin, *Romance and Rights: The Politics of Interracial Intimacy, 1945–1954* (Jackson: University of Mississippi Press, 2005), 116; Christine Knauer, *Let Us Fight as Free Men: Black Soldiers and Civil Rights* (Philadelphia: University of Pennsylvania Press, 2014), 153; Yasuhiro Okada, "'Cold War Black Orientalism': Race, Gender, and African American Representations of Japanese Women during the Early 1950s," *Journal of American & Canadian Studies*, no. 27 (Mar. 2009): 46–51; Michael Cullen Green, *Black Yanks in the Pacific: Race in the Making of American Military Empire after World War II* (Ithaca, NY: Cornell University Press, 2010), 61.

58 Klein, *Cold War Orientalism*, 28.

59 Lisa Yoneyama. "Liberation Under Siege: U.S. Military Occupation and Japanese Women's Enfranchisement." *American Quarterly* 57, No. 3 (2005).

60 Lily Anne Y. Welty Tamai, "Checking 'Other' Twice: Transnational Dual Minorities" in *Red & Yellow, Black & Brown: Decentering Whiteness in Mixed Race Studies*, ed. Joanne L. Rondilla, Rudy P. Guevarra Jr., and Paul Spickard (Newark, NJ: Rutgers University Press, 2017), 183–184.

61 Evelyn Nakano Glenn, "Issei, Nisei, Warbride: Three Generations of Japanese American Women in Domestic Service (Philadelphia: Temple University Press, 1986), 60–61.

62 Tolbert, Kathryn. "Japanese War Brides: An Oral History Archive." http://www.warbrideproject.com/.

63 Karen Kelsky, *Women on the Verge: Japanese Women, Western Dreams* (Durham, NC: Duke University Press, 2001) 2–3, 75.

64 Tolbert, Kathryn. "Japanese War Brides: An Oral History Archive." http://www.warbrideproject.com/.

65 Crockett, *Popcorn on the Ginza*, 131; Shibusawa, *America's Geisha Ally*, 35.

66 Gary Leupp, *Interracial Intimacy in Japan: Western Men and Japanese Women, 1543–1900* (London: Continuum, 2003), 53.

67 Leupp, 55.

68 Leisa D. Meyer, *Creating GI Jane: Sexuality and Power in the Women's Army Corps During World War II* (New York: Columbia University Press, 1996), 135.

69 Sylvia J. Rock. "Japan Intrigued Jersey Girl," *Baltimore Afro-American*, Oct 13, 1951.

70 "Jap Soldiers Replacing Tan Yanks as Laborers," *Baltimore Afro American*, Oct. 13, 1945.

71 Sylvia J. Rock. "Japan Intrigued Jersey Girl."

72 Yasuhiro Okada, "Negotiating Race," 72.

73 James McGrath Morris, *Eye on the Struggle: Ethel Payne, The First Lady of the Black Press* (New York, NY: HarperCollins, 2015), 62–67.

74 Okada, "Negotiating Race," 84.

75 George Brown to the NAACP, November 20, 1949, RG II, box G15, folder "Soldier Marriage," NAACP Papers, Library of Congress, Washington, DC.

76 Peggy Pascoe, 247; Zeiger, 169. Michael Cullen Green also cites George D. Brown's letter in his study of Afro-Asian intimacies in Occupied Japan. However, Green

draws a different conclusion. See *Black Yanks in the Pacific: Race in the Making of American Military Empire after World War II* (Ithaca, NY: Cornell University Press, 2010), 72–73.

77 Reiji Yoshida, "Letters from Kobe, Young Reckless, Open-Eyed GIs Broke Social Taboos, Found War Brides, Racist Laws, VD," *The Japan Times*, September 9, 2008.

78 Jack Greenberg (NAACP) to James C. Evans (Civilian Assistant, Office of the Secretary of Defense), December 1, 1949, RG II, Box G15, folder "Soldier Marriage," NAACP Papers, Library of Congress, Washington, DC.

79 James C. Evans (Civilian Assistant, Office of the Secretary of Defense) to Jack Greenberg (NAACP), December 23, 1949, RG II, Box G15, folder "Soldier Marriage," NAACP Papers, Library of Congress, Washington, DC.

80 Phillip McGuire, "Desegregation of the Armed Forces: Black Leadership, Protest, and World War II," *The Journal of Negro History* 68, no. 2 (Spring 1983): 147.

81 Yukiko Koshiro, *Trans-Pacific Racisms and the U.S. Occupation of Japan* (New York: Columbia University Press, 1999), 157; Walter Edwards, *Modern Japan Through its Weddings: Gender, Person, and Society in Ritual Portrayal*, (Stanford, CA: Stanford University Press, 1989), 103.

82 James C. Evans (Civilian Assistant, Office of the Secretary of Defense) to Jack Greenberg (NAACP), December 23, 1949, RG II, Box G15, folder "Soldier Marriage," NAACP Papers, Library of Congress, Washington, DC.

83 Jack Greenberg (NAACP) to Mr. George D. Brown, December 28, 1949. RG II, Box G15, folder "Soldier Marriage," NAACP Papers, Library of Congress, Washington, DC.

84 Zeiger, *Entangling Alliances*, 181.

85 L. Alex Wilson, "24th Infantry GI's Lovesick . . . 400 to Wed Tokyo Girls," *The Chicago Defender*, November 4, 1950.

86 Brenda Gayle Plummer, ed. "Brown Babies: Race, Gender and Policy after World War II." *Window on Freedom: Race, Civil Rights and Foreign Affairs, 1945–1988* (Chapel Hill: University of North Carolina Press, 2003), 67–91.

87 L. Alex Wilson, "Why Tan Yanks Go For Japanese Girls," *The Chicago Defender*, November 11, 1950.

88 Zeiger, *Entangling Alliances*, 170.

89 Robert Bradford to the NAACP, October 28, 1946, RG II, Box G15, NAACP Papers, Library of Congress, Washington, DC.

90 George Brown to NAACP, NAACP Papers.

91 Wilson, "24th Infantry GI's Lovesick."

92 W. E. B. DuBois, *The Souls of Black Folk* (New York: Avon Books, 1965), 9.

93 Walter White to Robert P. Patterson (Secretary of War, The War Department), December 20, 1945. Library of Congress, NAACP Papers, Part II: Veterans Affairs File, 1940–1950, Group II, Box G15, folder "Part II: Veterans Affairs," NAACP Papers, Library of Congress, Washington DC.

94 Pascoe, *What Comes Naturally*, 247.

95 Peter Wallenstein, *Tell the Court I Love My Wife: Race, Marriage, and Law—An American History* (New York: Palgrave Macmillan, 2002) 184.
96 Gardner, 14.

4. "A BRIDGE BETWEEN EAST AND WEST"

1 Mr. and Mrs. Andrew Radtke to Sidney R. Yates, February, 17, 1950, series 4, box 105, folder 11, Sidney R. Yates Papers, Chicago Historical Society.
2 Private Law 614, 81st Congress, June 28, 1950.
3 Sidney R. Yates to Thomas Radtke, July 28, 1950, series 4, box 105, folder 11, Sidney R. Yates Papers, Chicago Historical Society.
4 Bok-Lim C. Kim, "Asian Wives of US Servicemen: Women in Shadows," *Amerasia* 4, no.1, 99.
5 Naoko Shibusawa, *America's Geisha Ally: Reimagining the Japanese Enemy* (Cambridge, MA: Harvard University Press, 2006), 49; To learn more about the racial diversity of war bride husbands see, Romanzo Adams Social Research Laboratory (RASRL), 1953–1955, box 1, folders 14–22, group 2 (Wife, Japanese; Husband, non-Japanese), 1–67, War Brides Interview Project, University of Hawai'i, Manoa Libraries.
6 Philip E. Wolgin and Irene Bloemraad, "'Our Gratitude,'" 37.
7 Summary of Proceedings, Thirteenth Annual National Convention, The America Legion, October 18–21, 1948.
8 Martha Gardner, *The Qualities of a Citizen: Women, Immigration, and Citizenship, 1870–1965* (Princeton, NJ: Princeton University Press, 2005).
9 James T. Sparrow, *Warfare State: World War II Americans and the Age of Big Government* (New York: Oxford University Press, 2011), Chapter 6.
10 Philip E. Wolgin and Irene Bloemraad. "'Our Gratitude,'" 37.
11 Eithne Luibhéld, *Entry Denied: Controlling Sexuality at the Border* (Minneapolis: University of Minnesota Press, 2002), 59.
12 Gardner, *The Qualities of a Citizen*, 13.
13 Cynthia Enloe, Maneuvers: The International Politics of Militarizing Women's Lives (Berkeley: University of California Press, 2000), 156.
14 Ibid.
15 Gardner, *The Qualities of a Citizen*, 225.
16 Mrs. Kester L. Hastings to Mrs. John G. Fowler, "History of Brides' Schools," September 27, 1956, RG ANRC, box 1280, located at 130/78/38/06, file "War Brides, Japan, and Korea, Japanese War Bride' School," Records of the American National Red Cross, National Archives, College Park, MD.
17 Larry Sakamoto, "GIs' Japanese Wives Offered Schooling," *Pacific Stars and Stripes*, March 10, 1951. The American Red Cross also opened up bride schools in Korea during the Korean conflict when American servicemen and Korean women married in record numbers. See "Bride School at Yongsan," *Pacific Stars and Stripes*, June 8, 1964.

18 American Red Cross Far Eastern Area Brides' Schools, October 18, 1955, RG ANRC, box 1280, located at 130/78/38/06, file "War Brides, Japan, and Korea, Japanese War Bride' School," Records of the American National Red Cross, National Archives, College Park, MD.

19 Elaine Tyler May, *Homeward Bound: American Families in the Cold War Era* (New York: Basic Books, 1988), 5–6.

20 Gardner, *The Qualities of a Citizen*, 19.

21 American Red Cross Far Eastern Area Brides' Schools, October 18, 1955, RG ANRC, box 1280, located at 130/78/38/06, file "War Brides, Japan, and Korea, Japanese War Bride' School," Records of the American National Red Cross, National Archives, College Park, MD.

22 "Minutes of Meeting on Bride Schools," Washington Heights Civilian Club, August 19, 1957, RG ANRC, box 1280, located at 130/78/38/06, file "War Brides, Japan, and Korea, Japanese War Bride' School," Records of the American National Red Cross, National Archives, College Park, MD.

23 Michiko Takeuchi. "Cold War Manifest Domesticity: The "Kitchen Debate" and Single American Occupationnairre Women in the U.S. Occupation of Japan, 1945–1952." *US-Japan Women's Journal*, no. 50, 2016, 19.

24 Seung Ah Oh, "*Recontextualizing Asian American Domesticity: From Madame Butterfly to My American Wife!*" (Lanham, MD: Lexington Books, 2008), ix.

25 Masako Nakamura, "Families Precede Nation and Race?: Marriage, Migration, and Integration of Japanese War Brides after World War II." PhD diss, University of Minnesota, 2010, 76.

26 Mire Koikari. *Pedagogy of Democracy: Feminism and the Cold War in the U.S. Occupation of Japan* (Philadelphia: Temple University Press, 2008); Michiko Takeuchi. "Cold War Manifest Domesticity: The "Kitchen Debate" and Single American Occupationnaire Women in the U.S. Occupation of Japan, 1945–1952." *US-Japan Women's Journal*, no. 50, 2016; Lisa Yoneyama. "Liberation Under Siege: U.S. Military Occupation and Japanese Women's Enfranchisement." *American Quarterly* 57, no. 3 (2005).

27 Michiko Takeuchi, "Cold War Manifest Domesticity," 13.

28 Camp Kokura Brides School, American Red Cross, October, 1956, RG ANRC, box 1280, located at 130/78/38/06, file "War Brides, Japan, and Korea, Japanese War Bride' School," Records of the American National Red Cross, National Archives, College Park, MD.

29 Camp Kokura Brides School, American Red Cross, October, 1956, RG ANRC, box 1280, located at 130/78/38/06, file "War Brides, Japan, and Korea, Japanese War Bride' School," Records of the American National Red Cross, National Archives, College Park, MD.; For an extensive description of the bride school curriculum see Regina Lark, *They Challenged Two Nations: Marriages between Japanese Women and American GIs, 1945 to Present*, PhD Diss., University of Southern California, 1999, 238–286.

30 Stephen R. Porter, *Benevolent Empire: U.S. Power, Humanitarianism, and the World's Dispossessed* (Philadelphia: University of Pennsylvania Press, 2017), 78.

31 Porter, *Benevolent Empire*, 9.

32 Chizuko Tsutsumi, "Study of Japanese-American Intercultural Families," International Institute of San Francisco, 1961, RG ANRC, box 1280, located at 130/78/38/06, file "War Brides, Japan, and Korea, Japanese War Bride' School," Records of the American National Red Cross, National Archives, College Park, MD.

33 Mrs. Robert Whitelaw Wilson to Mrs. John G. fowler, Letter, Bride School Report, Camp Sendai. March 2, 1956, RG ANRC, box 1280, located at 130/78/38/06, file "War Brides, Japan, and Korea, Japanese War Bride' School," Records of the American National Red Cross, National Archives, College Park, MD.

34 Mrs. John G. Fowler to Mrs. Robert W. Wilson, letter, "Brides' Schools Publicity and Information, undated, RG ANRC, box 1280, located at 130/78/38/06, file "War Brides, Japan, and Korea, Japanese War Bride' School," Records of the American National Red Cross, National Archives, College Park, MD.

35 American Red Cross, Public Information Office, Tokyo, Japan, April 20, 1954, RG ANRC, box 1280, located at 130/78/38/06, file "War Brides, Japan, and Korea, Japanese War Bride' School," Records of the American National Red Cross, National Archives, College Park, MD.

36 Haru Matsukata Reischauer, "Talk to the first meeting of the American Red Cross Brides' School, By Mrs. Reischauer, Wife of the Ambassador to Japan." March, 1, 1963, RG ANRC, box 1280, located at 130/78/38/06, file "War Brides, Japan, and Korea, Japanese War Bride' School," Records of the American National Red Cross, National Archives, College Park, MD.

37 Bruce Weber, "Looking Back on a Life Divided Loyalties," *New York Times*, August, 24, 1996.

38 Susan Dibble, "Meet Mrs. Reischauer: Down to Earth Outlook at U.S. Embassy in Tokyo." *Pacific Stars and Stripes*, December 26, 1965.

39 Haru Matsukata Reischauer, "Talk to the first meeting of the American Red Cross Brides' School, By Mrs. Reischauer, Wife of the Ambassador to Japan." March 1, 1963, RG ANRC, box 1280, located at 130/78/38/06, file "War Brides, Japan, and Korea, Japanese War Bride' School," Records of the American National Red Cross, National Archives, College Park, MD.

40 Eiji Takemae, *The Allied Occupation of Japan*," (New York: Continuum, 2003), 498.

41 Ursula Vogel, "Marriage and the Boundaries of Citizenship," in Steenbergen, Bart, *The Condition of Citizenship* (London: SAGE Publications, 1994), 77.

42 Ursula Vogel, "Marriage and the Boundaries of Citizenship," 77.

43 Catherine Lee has argued, family reunification was a feature of immigration policy, at different periods, and for different groups, long before the Hart-Cellar Act of 1965. See Catherine Lee, *Fictive Kinship: Family Reunification and the Meaning of Race and Nation in American Immigration* (New York: Russell Sage Foundation,

2013). However, in some extreme cases, Japanese women were deported. For example, Etsuko Britton was ordered to return to Japan after she was convicted of manslaughter for strangling her young son in Chicago, Illinois in 1952.

44 Janet Wentworth Smith and William L. Worden, "They're Bringing Home Japanese Wives," *Saturday Evening Post*, January 19, 1952.

45 Elena Tajima Creef. "Discovering My Mother as the Other in *The Saturday Evening* Post." *Qualitative Inquiry* 6, no. 4, 451.

46 Howard Bryan, "Letters to the Editors," *Saturday Evening Post*, March 1, 1952.

47 Creef, "Discovering my Mother," notes her mother Chiyohi was never interviewed for the article, 443.

48 Creef, "Discovering my Mother," 449.

49 Ju Yon Kim, *The Racial Mundane: Asian American Performance and the Embodied Everyday* (New York: New York University Press, 2015), 100.

50 Seung Ah Oh, "*Recontextualizing Asian American Domesticity*," 59.

51 Edwin Andrews, "Orientation Program for Japanese National (Brides)," in author's possession.

52 Kathleen S. Uno, "The Death of 'Good Wife, Wise Mother'?" in *Postwar Japan as History* (Berkeley: University of California Press, 1993), 297.

53 Koyama Shizuko, *Ryōsai Kenbo: The Educational Ideal of 'Good Wife, Wise Mother' in Modern Japan* (Boston, MA: Brill, 2013), 7–8.

54 Masako Nakamura, "Families Precede Nation and Race?: Marriage, Migration, and Integration of Japanese War Brides After World War II" PhD Dissertation, University of Minnesota, 2010, 77. See also discussion of the "model-minority wife" in "Checking 'Other' Twice: Transnational Dual Minorities," in *Red and Yellow, Black and Brown: Decentering Whiteness in Mixed Race Studies* (New Brunswick, NJ: Rutgers University Press, 2017), 184.

55 May, *Homeward Bound*, 19.

56 The American Red Cross. "Introduction to the American Way of Life." A Course for Brides, Foreign Born Wives of American Servicemen, undated , RG ANRC, box 1280, located at 130/78/38/06, file "War Brides, Japan, and Korea, Japanese War Bride' School," Records of the American National Red Cross, National Archives, College Park, MD.

57 Klein, *Cold War Orientalism*, 28.

58 John Dower, *Embracing Defeat: Japan in the Wake of World War II* (New York: W. W. Norton & Co./The New Press, 1999), 133.

59 Naoko Shibusawa, *America's Geisha Ally*, 4.

60 Caroline Chung Simpson, *An Absent Presence: Japanese Americans in Postwar American Culture, 1945–1960* (Chapel Hill: University of Carolina Press, 2011), 183.

61 Shibusawa offers a more detailed analysis of *Sayonara* and other films in the genre. See Shibusawa, *America's Geisha Ally*, chapter seven, "Hollywood's Japan."

62 Maria Isabel Seguro, "Redeeming American Democracy in Sayonara," *Coolabah*, No. 5, 2011, *Observatori: Centre d'Estudis Australians, Austrialan Studies centre, Universitat de Barcelona*, 216.

63 Maria Isabel Seguro, "Redeeming American Democracy in Sayonara," 215; Caroline Chung Simpson, *An Absent Presence: Japanese Americans in Postwar American Culture, 1945–1960* (Chapel Hill: University of Carolina Press, 2011), 171–185.

64 Gina Marchetti, *Romance and the Yellow Peril: Race, Sex, and Discursive Strategies in Hollywood Fiction* (Berkeley: University of California Press, 1993), 158.

65 Mae Tinee, "Japanese War Bride Film has Punch, Pathos." *Chicago Daily Tribune*, February 4, 1952.

66 Marchetti, *Romance and the Yellow Peril*, 158.

67 Marchetti, *Romance and the Yellow Peril*, 78.

68 Audrey Amidon. "Favorite Film Finds of 2017." December 13, 2017. https://unwritten-record.blogs.archives.gov/2017/12/13/favorite-film-finds-of-2017/

69 dir. King Vidor, *Japanese Bride in America*, 1952, RG 306 A1 1098 Movie Scripts, 1942 – 1965, Box 20, located at: 230/47/17/03, File: Japanese Bride in America, National Archives Records and Administration, College Park, Maryland.

70 "GI and Japanese Wife Arrive to See his Parents," *Chicago Daily Tribune*, Nov 20, 1951.

5. GOODWILL AMBASSADORS

1 Ruth Moss, "Mother Slays Baby; Relates Tale of Abuse," *Chicago Daily Tribune*, November 15, 1953, 43.

2 "Japan War Wife Gets Mind Test for Child Killing," *Pacific Stars and Stripes*, January 2, 1954; "War Bride's Suicide Try Fails," *Pacific Starts and Stripes*, February 21, 1954; "Jap War Bride Charged With Slaying Son," *Cedar Rapids Gazette*, November 17. 1953

3 Alessandro Castellini, "Silent Voices: Mothers Who Kill Their Children and the Women's Liberation Movement in 1970s Japan," *Feminist Review* no.106 (2014).

4 Moss, *Mother Slays Baby.*

5 Shibusawa, *America's Geisha Ally*; Klein, *Cold War Orientalism.*

6 James A. Michener, "Pursuit of Happiness by a GI and a Japanese." *LIFE*, February 21, 1955, 132.

7 Michener, 135; Simpson, *An Absent Presence*, 180.

8 "Lobbying For Love," *Scene*, May, 1950. Japanese American Service Committee Legacy Center, Chicago, IL.

9 Carrol Klotzbach, "My Japanese Wife," *Scene*, July 1951, 22. Japanese American Service Committee Legacy Center, Chicago, IL.

10 Caroline Chung Simpson, "'Out of an Obscure Place': Japanese War Brides and Cultural Pluralism in the 1950s," *Differences: A Journal of feminist Cultural Studies* 10, no. 3 (1998): 70.

11 Mrs. James Durwin, "Story Was Heartwarming," letter to the editor, *Scene*, August 1951, 22. Japanese American Service Committee Legacy Center, Chicago, IL.

12 Vicki Ruiz, *From Out of the Shadows: Mexican Women in Twentieth-Century America* (New York: Oxford University Press, 2008), xiii.

13 Valerie J. Matsumoto, *City Girls: The Nisei Social World in Los Angeles, 1920–1950* (New York: Oxford University Press, 2014), 2.
14 "L. B. Japanese War Brides Form Club," *Independent Press Telegram*, April 15, 1956.
15 "Japanese War Brides Give Shower for Baby," *Albuquerque Tribune*, February 21, 1956.
16 "Japan Brides Club Studies U.S. Ways," *Pacific Stars and Stripes*, August 28, 1957.
17 "Japanese War Bride Plans Club," *Mansfield News Journal*, September 7, 1952.
18 "Chicago War Brides," *Scene*, July 1953. Japanese American Service Committee Legacy Center, Chicago, IL.
19 Chicago Resettlers Committee, Board meeting report, October 4, 1952. Japanese American Service Committee Legacy Center, Chicago, IL.
20 Glenda Elizabeth Gilmore, *Gender and Jim Crow: Women and the Politics of White Supremacy in North Carolina, 1896–1920* (Chapel Hill: The University of North Carolina Press, 1996), 148.
21 Gabe Faviona, "Club Helps Japanese War Brides Adjust," *Chicago Sun Times*, December 22, 1957; "War Brides' Club Seeks New Name," *Chicago Shimpo*, August 15, 1953.
22 "Chicago War Brides," *Scene*, July 1953, 39. Japanese American Service Committee Legacy Center, Chicago, IL.
23 Gabe Faviona, "Club Helps Japanese War Brides Adjust," *Chicago Sun Times*, December 22, 1957.
24 "Are War Brides Happy?" *Scene*, November 1954, 22. Japanese American Service Committee Legacy Center, Chicago, IL.
25 Tragic stories about Japanese war brides can be viewed in newspapers across the country. See Lynette Shifman, "Deserted War Bride Plight," *Los Angeles Times*, July 18, 1971, k2; "Abandons Japanese War Bride," *Daily Defender*, October 6, 1958, A2; "War Bride Tries to Kill Children, Self," *The Washington Post*, May, 19, 1957, A14.
26 "Are War Brides Happy?" *Scene*, November 1954, 22. Japanese American Service Committee Legacy Center, Chicago, IL.
27 "Japanese War Bride Seeks to Form Clubs To Aide East, West," *Corpus Christi Caller Times*, August 3, 1952.
28 Steven L. Davis, *Texas Literary Outlaws: Six Writers in the Sixties, and Beyond* (Fort Worth: Texas Christian University Press, 2004), 29.
29 "Repatriated Texan Speaks," *Sweetwater Reporter* (Sweetwater, Tex.), January 5, 1954.
30 Paul M. Edwards, *The Korean War: A Historical Dictionary* (Lanham, MD: Scarecrow Press, 2003), 77.
31 "Reconverted GI Cries at Reunion with Wife." *Los Angeles Times*, January 4, 1954.
32 "Texas G.I. Quits Red Camp," *Daily Boston Globe*, 1954.
33 Sandra Zeiger, *Entangling Alliances*, 197–202.
34 "The Loneliest Brides in America," *Ebony*, December 1953.
35 "The Truth About Japanese War Brides," *Ebony*, January 1952.

36 "The Loneliest Brides," 18.
37 "Letters to Editors," *Ebony*, March, 1953; "Letters to Editors," *Ebony*, April 1953.
38 Lily Anne Y. Welty Tamai, "Checking 'Other' Twice: Transnational Dual Minorities," in *Red and Yellow, Black and Brown: Decentering Whiteness in Mixed Race Studies* (New Brunswick, NJ: Rutgers University Press, 2017), 184.
39 "The Loneliest Brides" 23.
40 Ibid, 17.
41 Ibid, 18.
42 Takiko's grandson, Jerome White Jr., known to his fans as Jero, is a famous Black Japanese enka singer (enka is Japanese music born in the aftermath of World War II and has been likened to American country music in its content and blues in its sound) who speaks highly of his grandmother and her influence in his life. Born and raised in Pittsburgh, Pennsylvania, White credits his grandmother Takiko for his successful career as an enka singer because it was she who first introduced him to enka, the music of her generation, when he was just a child. See: Blaine Hardin, "A Far Cry From Home," *The Washington Post*, May 28, 2008; Michael E Ruane, "Festival Feature: A Japanese Idol From Pittsburgh," *The Washington Post*, March 28, 2009; Chris Yeager, "Jero: Japan's First African-American Enka Singer," *Japan America Society of Greater Philadelphia, Konnichiwa Philadelphia*, July 2, 2008.
43 Setsuko Williams (pseudonym used), interviewed by author, Marin City, CA, July 7, 2010.
44 Ibid.
45 When Setsuko talked about the racial violence in Dallas, she specifically recalled a Black church bombing by hostile whites. However, I was unable to locate any sound evidence that a church bombing had occurred in Dallas in the few years Setsuko was living there.
46 Shibusawa, *America's Geisha Ally*, 50.
47 Anthony Brown, "Sumi's Story," from the Brown family personal collection, unpublished, in author's possession.
48 Ngai, *Impossible Subjects*, 175.
49 Susan Skolnick, "'War Brides' Relate their Shared Trauma," *Asian Week* 6, no. 32 (April 5, 1988):18.
50 Chizuko Tsutsumi, in the "File for those who work with the Japanese wives of American citizens and their families," A Rosenberg Foundation Project of the International Institute of San Francisco, 1962. Part of a personal collection owned by an affiliate of the Institute, Ms. Kazuko Tsuchiya. For this study the Institute interviewed one hundred Japanese war brides in the San Francisco Bay area.
51 Anthony Brown, "Sumi's Story," From the Brown family personal collection, unpublished. In Sumi's story, Mac goes on to explain to Willie Brown about the racial hostilities particular to Japantown. Brown writes, "Mac said that after Japanesetown was evacuated [referring to Japanese Internment], it was a ghost town. The Government tried to sell the property but no white folks wanted to

move in. So they rented it out to all the colored folks who were recruited out of the ports and docks in Gulf States like Louisiana, Mississippi, and Texas, to come work in the shipyards here for the war. So when the Japanese folks got out of the camps and came back to Japanesetown, many were greeted at the door of their old homes by colored faces."

52 Helen M. Day, "Baby-San Becoming Mrs. American," box 19–15, "Japanese War Brides, 1955–1957," International Institute of Metropolitan Detroit Collection Records, Walter P. Reuther Library of Labor and Urban Affairs, Wayne State University.

53 Chizuko Tsutsumi, "File for those who work with the Japanese wives of American citizens and their families," A Rosenberg Foundation Project of the International Institute of San Francisco, 1962, 5.

54 See chapter 4, page 16 in Marian Mizuno, "Report on the Japanese War Bride Survey," December 1956, box 19–15, "Japanese War Brides, 1955–1957," International Institute of Metropolitan Detroit Collection Records, Walter P. Reuther Library of Labor and Urban Affairs, Wayne State University.

55 "The Loneliest Brides in America," *Ebony*, January 1953, 17.

56 Interview with Japanese War Bride A-18, January 27, 1954, Romanzo Adams Social Research Laboratory (RASRL), 1953–1955, box 1, folders 14–22, group 2 (Wife, Japanese; Husband, non-Japanese), 1–67, War Brides Interview Project, University of Hawai'i, Manoa Libraries.

57 Creef, "Discovering My Mother," 446; Japanese war brides also tended to excluded women who married servicemen of low rank.

58 Williams, interviewed 2010.

59 Like the Issei and Nisei, Japanese war brides gave their children "American" names. This was a strident effort to distract others of their mixed-Japanese backgrounds. Sumi Brown's son, Anthony, told me in conversation that his parent's gave him and his brothers non-Japanese names in an attempt to downplay their Japanese heritage so the boys would get along better in life.

60 Dana Perrigan, "Marin City Looks to Better days," *The San Francisco Chronicle*, March 15, 2009, N-4.

61 Obituary for "Brown, Sumi" *San Francisco Chronicle*, July 10, 2010.

62 James T. Sparrow, *Warfare State: World War II Americans and the Age of Big Government* (New York: Oxford University Press, 2011), Chapter 6.

63 Philip E. Wolgin and Irene Bloemraad. "'Our Gratitude,'" 37.

64 Ibid., 27.

EPILOGUE

1 Briones, *Jim and Jap Crow*, 5.

2 Nicole Constable, "The Commodification of Intimacy: Marriage, Sex, and Reproductive Labor," *Annual Review of Anthropology* 38 (2009): 50.

3 Personal communication with author.

4 Welty Tamai, "Checking 'Other' Twice," 4.; Joanne L. Rondilla et al, *Red & Yellow, Black & Brown*, 7.

5 Joanne L. Rondilla et al, *Red & Yellow, Black & Brown*, 7.

6 Kim M. Williams, "Linking the Civil Rights and Multiracial Movements," in *The Politics of Multiracialism: Challenging Racial Thinking*, Heather M. Dalmage, ed. (Albany: State University of New York Press, 2004).

7 Mark Brilliant, *The Color of America Has Changed: How Racial Diversity Shaped Civil Rights Reform in California, 1941–1978* (Oxford: Oxford University Press, 2010).

8 Blaine Hardin, "A Far Cry From Home," *The Washington Post*, May 28, 2008; Michael E Ruane, "Festival Feature: A Japanese Idol From Pittsburgh," *The Washington Post*, March 28, 2009; Chris Yeager, "Jero: Japan's First African–American Enka Singer," Japan America Society of Greater Philadelphia, *Konnichiwa Philadelphia*, July 2, 2008.

9 Jero's popularity might also be suggestive of modern Japan's fetishization of Blackness. Yuya Kiuchi, "An Alternative African-America Image in Japan: Jero as a Cross-generational Bridge between Japan and the United States," *Journal of Popular Culture* 42, no. 3 (2009).

10 Jhene Aiko, a popular singer and songwriter, is of Japanese and Black descent, and Preston Oshita, a Chicago-based rapper that goes by the name "Towkio," is of Japanese and Mexican descent.

11 For more on military, intimacy, and multiracialism, see Beth Bailey and David Farber, *The First Strange Place: Race and Sex in World War II Hawaii* (Baltimore, MD: John Hopkins University Press, 1992); *Racial Beachhead: Diversity and Democracy in a Military Town: Seaside, California*. (Stanford, CA: Stanford University Press, 2012). For more on intimacy, military, and immigration, see Ji-Yeon Yuh, *Beyond the Shadow of Camptown: Korean Military Brides in America* (New York: New York University Press, 2002).

12 *In Racial Beachhead: Diversity and Democracy in a Military Town*, Carol Lynn McKibben argues that in the town of Seaside, a small community created to house and serve the neighboring US military base of Fort Ord, the multiracial population has successfully created a racially inclusive community and thus serves as a model for inclusion. See McKibben, *Racial Beachhead*.

13 Naoko Shibusawa, *America's Geisha Ally: Reimagining the Japanese Enemy* (Cambridge, MA: Harvard University Press, 2006), 375.

14 Jo Guldi and David Armitage, *The History Manifesto* (Cambridge, UK: Cambridge University Press, 2014).

15 Marion F. Houstoun, Riger G. Kramer, and Joan Mackin Barrett, "Female Predominance in Immigration to the United States Since 1930s: A First Look," *The International Migration Review* 18, no. 4 (1984).

16 Catherine Lee. "Where the Danger Lies": Race, Gender, and Chinese and Japanese Exclusion in the United States, 1870–1924" *Sociological Forum* 25, no. 2 (June 2010).

BIBLIOGRAPHY

MANUSCRIPT COLLECTIONS AND ARCHIVAL SOURCES

Case Files, Japanese American Service Committee (JASC), Chicago, IL

Crew Lists of Vessels Arriving at Seattle, Washington, 19031917, National Archives and Records Administration, Washington, DC

International Institute of Metropolitan Detroit Collection Records, Walter P. Reuther Library of Labor and Urban Affairs, Wayne State University

Japanese American Project. California State University, Fullerton Oral History Program

John Powell Irish Papers, Department of Special Collections, Stanford University Libraries

National Association for the Advancement of Colored People (NAACP) Papers, Library of Congress, Washington, DC

National Immigration Arrival Investigation Files, National Archives and Records Administration, San Bruno, CA

Papers Relating to the *Foreign Relations of the United States*, US Department of State, Office of the Historian, Washington, DC

Records of the American National Red Cross, National Archives and Records Administration, College Park, MD

Records of the War Relocation Authority, National Archives and Records Administration, College Park, MD

Ross Harano Papers and Photograph Collection, Japanese American Service Committee (JASC), Chicago, IL

Survey of Race Relation Records, Hoover Institution Archives, Stanford University

Tsutsumi, Chizuko. "File for those who work with the Japanese wives of American citizens and their families," A Rosenberg Foundation Project of the International Institute of San Francisco, 1962. Personal collection of Ms. Kazuko Tsuchiya.

US Census Bureau, National Archives and Records Administration, Washington, DC

US Selective Service System, National Archives and Records Administration, Washington, DC

War Brides Interview Project, University of Hawai'i, Manoa Libraries

PUBLISHED PRIMARY AND SECONDARY SOURCES

Albuquerque Tribune. "Japanese War Brides Give Shower for Baby." February 21, 1956.

Almaguer, Tomas. "Racial Domination and Class Conflict in Capitalist Agriculture: The Oxnard Sugar Beet Workers Strike of 1903." *Labor History* 25, no. 3 (Summer 1984).

———. *Racial Fault Lines: The Historical Origins of White Supremacy in California*. Berkeley: University of California Press, 1994.

Asaka, Ikuko. "'Colored Men of the East': African Americans and the Instability of Race in US-Japan Relations." *American Quarterly* 66, no. 4 (December 2014).

Ayukawa, Midge. "Good Wives and Wise Mothers: Japanese Picture Brides in Early Twentieth-Century British Columbia," *BC Studies*, no.105–106 (Spring/Summer 1995).

Azuma, Eiichiro. *Between Two Empires: Race, History, and Transnationalism in Japanese America*. Oxford: Oxford University Press, 2005.

Bailey, Beth and David Farber. *The First Strange Place: Race and Sex in World War II Hawaii*. Baltimore, MD: John Hopkins University Press, 1992.

Baltimore Afro-American (1893–1988). "3-Year Courtship in Japan: Baltimore GI, Tokyo Bride, Find Love Is All Languages." April 26, 1952.

———. "Americans Make Themselves at Home in Japan." April 17, 1948.

———. "Jap Soldiers Replacing Tan Yanks as Laborers." October 13, 1945.

———. "Japan Intrigued Jersey Girl." October 13, 1951.

———. "Trenton Man Named U.S. Officer." October 4, 1952.

Bannister, Robert C. "Dorothy Swain Thomas: Soziologischer Objectivismus: Der Harte Weg in die Profession." In *Frauen in der Soziologie: Neun Portrats*, ed. Claudia Honegger und Teresa Wobbe. Munich: C.H. Beck, 1998.

Bilbo, Theodore Gilmore. *Take Your Choice: Separation or Mongrelization*. Poplarville, MS: Dream House Publishing Company, 1947.

Boston Globe Magazine. "Japanese Women." November 25, 1917.

Bowers, William, William M. Hammond and George L. MacGarrigle. *Black Soldier, White Army: The 24th Infantry Regiment in Korea*. Washington, DC: Center for Military History.

Brilliant, Mark. *The Color of America Has Changed: How Racial Diversity Shaped Civil Rights Reform in California, 1941–1978*. Oxford: Oxford University Press, 2010.

Briones, Matthew. *Jim and Jap Crow: A Cultural History of the 1940s Interracial America*. Princeton: Princeton University Press, 2012.

Burns, Deborah Meiko King. "A Brief History of the JASC." The Japanese American Service Committee Legacy Center. Chicago, IL, 1989.

Butler, Maurice. *Out from the Shadow: The Story of Charles L. Glittens Who Broke the Color Barrier in the United States Secret Service*. Washington, DC: Xlibris Publishing, 2012.

Carter, Vednita and Evelina Giobbe. "Duet: Prostitution, Racism, and Feminist Discourse," in "Economic Justice for Sex," symposium issue, *Hastings Women's Law Journal* 1, no. 1 (1999).

Castellini, Alessandro. "Silent Voices: Mothers Who Kill Their Children and the Women's Liberation Movement in 1970s Japan." *Feminist Review* no.106 (2014).

Caswell, Michelle. *Archiving the Unspeakable: Silence, Memory, and the Photographic Record in Cambodia*. Madison: University of Wisconsin Press, 2014.

———. "Seeing Yourself in History: Community Archives and the Fight Against Symbolic Annihilation," *The Public Historian* 36, no. 4 (November 2014).

Chicago Daily Tribune (1923–1963). "GI and Japanese Wife Arrive to See His Parents." November 20, 1951.
Chicago Defender. "Court Martial Trials." October 14, 1944.
———. "Reader Tells of Race Violence in Japan." July 6, 1946.
Chicago Shimpo. "War Brides' Club Seeks New Name." August 15, 1953.
Chudacoff, Howard. *The Age of the Bachelor: Creating and American Subculture*. Princeton: Princeton University Press, 1999.
Constable, Nicole. "The Commodification of Intimacy: Marriage, Sex, and Reproductive Labor." *Annual Review of Anthropology* 38 (2009).
Corpus Christi Caller Times. "Japanese War Bride Seeks to Form Clubs to Aide East, West." August 3, 1952.
Cott, Nancy. *Public Vows: A History of Marriage and the Nation*. Cambridge, MA: Harvard University Press, 2000.
Creef, Elena Tajima. "Discovering My Mother as the Other in the Saturday Evening Post." *Qualitative Inquiry* 6, no. 4 (December 2000).
Daily Boston Globe. "Texas G.I. Quits Red Camp." 1954.
Daily Defender. "Abandons Japanese War Bride." October 6, 1958.
Dalmage, Heather M. *The Politics Of Multiracialism: Challenging Racial Thinking*. Albany: State University of New York Press, 2004.
Daniels, Roger. *The Politics of Prejudice: The Anti-Japanese Movement in California and the Struggle for Japanese Exclusion*. Berkeley: University of California Press, 1977.
Davis, Steven. *Texas Literary Outlaws: Six Writers in the Sixties and Beyond*. Fort Worth: Texas Christian University Press, 2004.
De Vos, George and Hiroshi Wagatsuma. *Japan's Invisible Race: Caste in Culture and Personality*. Berkeley: University of California Press, 1967.
Dower, John. *Embracing Defeat: Japan in the Wake of World War II*. New York: W.W. Norton & Company, 1999.
———. *War Without Mercy: Race and Power in the Pacific War*. New York: Pantheon Books, 1986.
Du Bois, W. E. B. "Forum Facet and Opinion." *Pittsburgh Courier*, March 20, 1937, 10.
———. *The Souls of Black Folk*. New York: Avon Books, (1903) 1965.
Duckett, Alfred. "Japs Teach Americans Democracy, GI Reports." *Baltimore Afro-American* (1893–1988), April 22, 1950.
Durwin, Mrs. James. "Story Was Heartwarming," letter to the editor. *Scene*, August 1951, 22. Japanese American Service Committee Legacy Center, Chicago, IL.
Ebony. "The Loneliest Brides in America." December 1953.
———. "The Truth About Japanese War Brides." January 1952.
Edwards, Paul. *The Korean War: A Historical Dictionary*. Lanham, MD: Scarecrow Press, 2003.
Edwards, Walter. *Modern Japan Through its Weddings: Gender, Person, and Society in Ritual Portrayal*. Stanford, CA: Stanford University Press, 1989.
Eiji, Takemae. *Inside the GHQ: The Allied Occupation of Japan and Its Legacy*. New York: Continuum, 2002.

Espiritu, Yen Le. *Asian American Women and Men*. Thousand Oaks, CA: Sage Publications, 1997.

———. *Homebound: Filipino American Lives Across Cultures, Communities, and Countries*. Berkeley: University of California Press, 2003.

Faviona, Gabe. "Club Helps Japanese War Brides Adjust." *Chicago Sun Times*, December 22, 1957.

Fugita, Stephen and Marilyn Fernandez. *Altered Lives, Enduring Community: Japanese Americans Remember Their World War II Incarceration*. Seattle: University of Washington Press, 2004.

Gallicchio, Marc S. *The African American Encounter with Japan and China Black Internationalism in Asia, 1895–1945*. Chapel Hill: University of North Carolina Press, 2000.

Gardner, Martha. *The Qualities of a Citizen: Women, Immigration, and Citizenship, 1870–1965*. Princeton: Princeton University Press, 2005.

Gee, Jennifer. "Housewives, Men's Villages, and Sexual Respectability: Gender and the Interrogation of Asian Women at the Angel Island Immigration Station." In *Asian/ Pacific Islander American Women*, edited by Shirley Hune and Gail M. Nomura. New York: New York University Press, 2003.

Geiger, Sandra. *Subverting Exclusion: Transpacifc Encounters with Race, Caste, and Borders, 1885–1928*. New Haven, CT: Yale University Press, 2011.

Gerbner, George and Larry Gross. "Living with Television: The Violence of Profile," *Journal of Communication* 26, no. 2 (Spring 1976).

Gilmore, Glenda Elizabeth. *Gender and Jim Crow: Women and the Politics of White Supremacy in North Carolina, 1896–1920*. Chapel Hill: The University of North Carolina Press, 1992.

Glenn, Evelyn Nakano. *Issei, Nisei, Warbride: Three Generations of Japanese American Women in Domestic Service*. Philadelphia: Temple University Press, 1986.

———. *Unequal Freedom: How Race and Gender Shaped American Citizenship and Labor*. Cambridge, MA: Harvard University Press, 2002.

Green, Michael Cullen. *Black Yanks in the Pacific: Race in the Making of American Military Empire after World War II*. Ithaca, NY: Cornell University Press, 2010.

Hardin, Blaine. "A Far Cry From Home." *Washington Post*, May 28, 2008.

Herdt, Gilbert, ed., *Moral Panics, Sex Panics: Fear and the Fight Over Sexual Rights*. New York: New York University Press, 2009.

Herndon Crockett, Lucy. *Popcorn on the Ginza: An Informal Portrait of Postwar Japan*, London: Victor Gollancz Ltd, 1949.

Hildegard, Lee. "A 'Child of Jazz' Bridges Fillmore and Japantown." *San Francisco Chronicle*, September 10, 2008.

Hisashi, Tsurutani. "America-Bound: The Japanese and the Opening of the American West," trans. Betsey Scheiner and Yamamura Mariko. Tokyo: *The Japan Times*, 1989.

Hondagneu-Sotelo, Pierrette. *Gendered Transitions: Mexican Experiences of Immigration*. Berkeley: University of California Press, 1994.

Horne, Gerald. *Facing the Rising Sun: African Americans, Japan, and the Rise of Afro-Asian Solidarity*. New York: New York University Press, 2018.

———. *Race War: White Supremacy and the Japanese Attack on the British Empire*. New York: New York University Press, 2004.

———. "Tokyo Bound: African Americans and Japan Confront White Supremacy" in "Blacks and Asians: Revisiting Racial Formations," special issue, *Souls: A Critical Journal in Black Politics, Culture, and Society* 3, no. 3 (Summer 2001).

Houstoun, Marion F., Riger G. Kramer, and Joan Mackin Barrett. "Female Predominance in Immigration to the United States Since 1930s: A First Look," *The International Migration Review* 18, no. 4 (1984).

Ichihashi, Yamato. *Japanese in the United States*. Stanford, CA: Stanford University Press, 1932.

Ichioka, Yuji. "Amerika Nadeshiko: Japanese Immigrant Women in the United States, 1900–1924." *Pacific Historical Review* 49, no. 2 (1980).

———. "Ameyuki-san: Japanese Prostitutes in Nineteenth-Century America." *Amerasia Journal* 4, no. 1 (1977).

———. *The Issei: The World of the First Generation Japanese Immigrants, 1885–1924*. New York: The Free Press, 1988.

———. *Views From Within: The Japanese American Evacuation and Resettlement Study*. Los Angeles: University of California Press, 1989.

Independent Press Telegram. "L. B. Japanese War Brides Form Club." April 15, 1956.

Iseman, Myre St. Wald, *Race Suicide*, New York: The Cosmopolitan Press, 1912.

Kearney, Reginald. "The Pro-Japanese Utterances of W. E. B. Du Bois," *Contributions in Black Studies* 13, no. 7 (1995).

Kelsky, Karen. *Women on the Verge: Japanese Women, Western Dreams*. Durham, NC: Duke University Press, 2001.

Kim, Bok-Lim C. "Asian Wives of U.S. Servicemen: Women in Shadows," *Amerasia Journal* 4, no. 1 (1977).

Klein, Christina. *Cold War Orientalism: Asia in the Middlebrow Imagination, 1945–1961*. Berkeley: University of California Press, 2003.

Klotzbach, Carrol. "My Japanese Wife," *Scene*, July 1951, 22. Japanese American Service Committee Legacy Center, Chicago, IL.

Knauer, Christine. *Let Us Fight as Free Men: Black Soldiers and Civil Rights*. Philadelphia: University of Pennsylvania Press, 2014.

Knepper, Cathy D. *Jersey Justice: The Story of the Trenton Six*. New Brunswick, NJ: Rivergate Books, 2011.

Koshiro, Yukiko. *Transpacific Racisms and the U.S. Occupation of Japan*. New York: Columbia University Press, 1999.

Kovner, Sarah. *Occupying Power: Sex Workers and Servicemen in Postwar Japan*. Stanford, CA: Stanford University Press, 2012.

Kuo, Karen. "'Japanese Women Are Like Volcanoes': Trans-Pacific Feminist Musings in Etsu I. Sugimoto's *A Daughter of the Samurai*." *Frontiers* 36, no. 1 (2015).

Lee, Catherine. "'Where the Danger Lies': Race, Gender, and Chinese and Japanese Exclusion in the United States, 1870–1924." *Sociological Forum* 25, no. 2 (2010).

Lee, Erika. *At America's Gates: Chinese Immigration During the Exclusion Era, 1892–1943*. Chapel Hill: University of North Carolina Press, 2003.

Levine, Lawrence. *Black Culture and Black Consciousness: Afro-American Folk Thought from Slavery to Freedom*. New York: Oxford University Press, 2007.

Leupp, Gary. *Interracial Intimacy in Japan: Western Men and Japanese Women, 1543–1900*. London: Continuum, 2003.

Literary Digest. "Japanese "Picture Brides" Become Frights in California." August 9, 1919.

Lipsitz, George. "'Frantic to Join . . . the Japanese Army': Black Soldiers and Civilians Confront the Asia-Pacific War." In *Perilous Memories: The Asia-Pacific War(s)*, eds. T. Fujitani, Geoffrey M. White, and Lisa Yoneyama. Durham, NC: Duke University Press, 2001.

Los Angeles Times. "Reconverted GI Cries at Reunion with Wife." Jan 4, 1954.

Lu, Sidney Xu. *The Making of Japanese Settler Colonialism: Malthusianism and Trans-Pacific Migration, 1868–1961*. Cambridge, UK: Cambridge University Press, 2019.

Lubin, Alex. *Romance and Rights: The Politics of Interracial Intimacy, 1945–1954*. Jackson: University of Mississippi Press, 2005.

Luibhéid, Eithne. *Entry Denied: Controlling Sexuality at the Border*. Minneapolis: University of Minnesota Press, 2002.

Marchetti, Gina. *Romance and the Yellow Peril: Race, Sex, and Discursive Strategies in Hollywood Fiction*. Berkeley: University of California Press, 1993.

Mansfield News Journal. "Japanese War Bride Plans Club." September 7, 1952.

Matsumoto, Valerie J. *City Girls: The Nisei Social World in Los Angeles, 1920–1950*. New York: Oxford University Press, 2014.

May, Elaine Tyler. *Homeward Bound: American families in the Cold War Era*. New York: Basic Books, 1988.

McGuire, Phillip. "Desegregation of the Armed Forces: Black Leadership, Protest, and World War II." *The Journal of Negro History* 68, no. 2 (Spring 1983).

McKibben, Carol Lynn. Racial Beachhead Diversity and Democracy in a Military Town. Stanford, CA: Stanford University Press, 2011.

Meger, Amy Lowe. *Historic Resource Study: Minidoka Internment National Monument*. National Park Service, US Department of the Interior. Seattle, WA, 2005.

Meyer, Leisa. *Creating GI Jane: Sexuality and Power in the Women's Army Corps During World War II*. New York: Columbia University Press, 1996.

Michener, James A. "Pursuit of Happiness by a GI and a Japanese." *LIFE*, February 21, 1955, 132.

Morris, James McGrath. *Eye on the Struggle: Ethel Payne, The First Lady of the Black Press*. New York: Harper Collins, 2015.

Moss, Ruth. "Mother Slays Baby; Relates Tale of Abuse." *Chicago Daily Tribune*, November 15, 1953.

Nakamura, Kelli Y. "Issei Women and Work: Washerwomen, Prostitutes, Midwives, and Barbers." *The Hawaiian Journal of History* 49 (2015).

Nakamura, Masako. "Families Precede Nation and Race?: Marriage, Migration, and Integration of Japanese War Brides After World War II," (PhD diss., University of Minnesota, 2010).

New York Times. "Chaplains' Aid Asked to End Fraternizing." April 3, 1946.

———. "GI Fraternization Allowed in Japan," July 12, 1946.

New York Tribune. "No More Babies in 2015." December 31, 1910.

Ngai, Mae. *Impossible Subjects: Illegal Aliens and the Making of Modern America*. Princeton: Princeton University Press, 2004.

Oguma, Eiji and David Askew, trans. *A Genealogy of Japanese Self-images*. Melbourne, Australia: Transpacific Press, 2002.

Oharazeki, Kazuhiro. "Anti-prostitution Campaigns in Japan and the American West, 1890–1920: A Transpacific Comparison." *Pacific Historical Review* 82, no. 2 (May 2013).

———. "Listening to the Voices of 'Other' Women in Japanese North America: Japanese Prostitutes and Barmaids in the American North West, 1887–1920," *Journal of American Ethnic History* 32, no. 4 (Summer 2013).

Okada, Yasuhiro. "'Cold War Black Orientalism': Race, Gender, and African American Representations of Japanese Women during the Early 1950s." *Journal of American & Canadian Studies*, no. 27 (March 2009).

———. "Negotiating Race and Womanhood Across the Pacific: African American Women in Japan under U.S. Military Occupation, 1945–1952." *Black Women, Gender, and Families* 6, no. 1 (Spring 2012).

Okado, Masakatsu. "The Women of Rural Japan: An Overview of the Twentieth Century," in *Farmers and Village Life in Japan*, ed. Ann Waswo and Nishida Yoshiaki. London: Routledge, 2003, 41–43.

Onishi, Yuichiro. *Transpacific Antiracism: Afro-Asian Solidarity in 20th-Century Black America, Japan, and Okinawa*. New York: New York University Press, 2013.

Pacific Stars and Stripes. "Bride School at Yongsan." June 8, 1964.

———. "Japan Brides Club Studies U.S. Ways," August 28, 1957.

Park, Robert E. "Human Migration and the Marginal Man." *American Journal of Sociology* 33, no. 6 (May 1928).

Pascoe, Peggy. *What Comes Naturally: Miscegenation Law and the Making of Race in America*. Oxford: Oxford University Press, 2009.

Perrigan, Dana. "Marin City looks to better days," *San Francisco Chronicle*, March 15, 2009.

Plummer, Brenda Gayle, ed. "Brown Babies: Race, Gender and Policy after World War II." *Window on Freedom: Race, Civil Rights and Foreign Affairs, 1945–1988*. Chapel Hill: University of North Carolina Press, 2003.

Porter, Stephen. *Benevolent Empire: U.S. Power, Humanitarianism, and the World's Dispossessed*. Philadelphia: University of Pennsylvania Press, 2017.

Rasmussen, Cecilia. "Hilltop Grave May Become a Shrine," *Los Angeles Times*, June 10, 2007.

Reddy, Vanita Reddy and Anantha Sudhakar. "Introduction: Feminist and Queer Afro-Asian Formations." *The Scholar and Feminist* 14, no. 3 (2018).

Reed, Christopher. *Bachelor Japanists: Japanese Aesthetics and Western Cultures*. New York: Columbia University Press, 2017.

Roberts, Mary Louise. *What Soldiers Do: Sex and the American GI in World War II France*. Chicago: University of Chicago Press, 2013.

Robinson, Greg. *The Great Unknown: Japanese American Sketches*. Boulder: University Press of Colorado, 2016.

Rondilla, Joanne L, Rudy P. Guevarra Jr., and Paul Spickard, eds. *Red & Yellow, Black & Brown: Decentering Whiteness in Mixed Race Studies*. Newark, NJ: Rutgers University Press, 2017.

Ruane, Michael E. "Festival Feature: A Japanese Idol From Pittsburgh," *Washington Post*, March 28, 2009.

Ruiz, Vicki. *From Out of the Shadows: Mexican Women in Twentieth-Century America.* Oxford: Oxford University Press, 2008.

San Francisco Chronicle. "Governor Asks US Action to Bar Japanese." June 22, 1920.

———. "Immoral Japanese." April 6, 1893.

———. "Immoral Japanese: Two Girls Who Will Be Sent Home." March 30, 1890.

———. "Japanese A Menace to American Women." March 1, 1905.

———. "Japan Violating Gentlemen's Pact Declares Hayes." January 20, 1917.

———. "Obituary for Brown, Sumi." July 10, 2010.

———. "Why Brown Men are a Dire Menace." April 10, 1905.

Sakamoto, Larry. "GIs' Japanese Wives Offered Schooling." *Pacific Stars and Stripes*, March 10, 1951.

Sawada, Mitziko. *Tokyo Life, New York Dreams: Urban Japanese Visions of America, 1890–1924*. Berkeley: University of California Press, 1996.

Scene. "Are War Brides Happy?" November 1954, 22. Japanese American Service Committee Legacy Center, Chicago, IL.

———. "Chicago War Brides." July 1953. Japanese American Service Committee Legacy Center, Chicago, IL.

———. "Lobbying For Love," May, 1950. Japanese American Service Committee Legacy Center, Chicago, IL.

Seguro, Maria Isabel. "Redeeming American Democracy in Sayonara." *Coolabah* no. 5 (2011). *Observatori: Centre d'Estudis Australians, Austrialan Studies centre, Universitat de Barcelona.*

Shibusawa, Naoko. *America's Geisha Ally: Reimagining the Japanese Enemy*. Cambridge, MA: Harvard University Press, 2006.

Shifman, Lynette. "Deserted War Bride Plight." *Los Angeles Times*, July 18, 1971.

Shigematsu, Stephen Murphy. *When Half Is Whole: Multiethnic Asian American Identities*. Stanford, CA: Stanford University Press, 2012.

Shukert, Elfrieda and Barbara Scibetta. *War Brides of World War II*. Novato, CA: Presidio Press, 1988.

Simpson, Caroline Chung. *An Absent Presence: Japanese Americans in Postwar American Culture, 1945–1960*. Durham: University of North Carolina Press, 2011.

Skolnick, Susan. "'War Brides' relate their shared trauma." *Asian Week* 6, no. 32 (April 5, 1988): 18.

Sparrow, James. *Warfare State: World War II Americans and the Age of Big Government*. New York: Oxford University Press, 2011.

Spickard, Paul. *Mixed Blood: Intermarriage and Ethnic Identity in 20th-Century America*. Madison: University of Wisconsin Press, 1989.

State Board of Control, California. California and the Oriental: Japanese, Chinese and Hindus. Report of State Board of Control of California to Gov. William D. Stephens, 1922.

Steiner, Jesse Frederick. *The Japanese Invasion: A Study in The Psychology of Inter-Racial Contacts*. Chicago: A. C. McClurg & Co., 1917.

Sueyoshi, Amy. *Queer Compulsions: Race, Nation, and Sexuality in the Affairs of Yone Noguchi*. Honolulu: University of Hawai'i Press, 2012.

Suzuki, Masao. "Success Story? Japanese Immigrant Economic Achievement and Return Migration, 1920–1930," *The Journal of Economic History* 55, no. 4 (December 1995).

Sweetwater Reporter. "Repatriated Texan Speaks." January 5, 1954.

Takemoto, Tina. "Looking for Jiro Onuma: A Queer Meditation on the Incarceration of Japanese Americans during World War II." *GLQ: A Journal of Lesbian And Gay Studies* 20, no. 3 (2014).

Tamai, Lilly Welty. "Checking "Other" Twice: Transnational Dual Minorities." In *Red and Yellow, Black and Brown: Decentering Whiteness in Mixed Race Studies*. New Brunswick, NJ: Rutgers University Press, 2017.

Teng, Emma. *Eurasian: Mixed Identities in the United States, China, and Hong Kong, 1842–1943*. Berkeley: University of California Press, 2013.

Throckmorton, J. M. "What The People Think: GI Reports Japan Doesn't Know Jim Crow." *The Pittsburgh Courier*, February 26, 1949.

Tinee, Mae. "Japanese War Bride Film has Punch, Pathos." *Chicago Daily Tribune (1923–1963)*, February 4, 1952.

Tolbert, Kathryn. "Japanese War Brides: An Oral History Archive," Accessed April 2018. http://www.warbrideproject.com/.

Tsu, Cecilia. "Sex, Lies, and Agriculture: Reconstructing Japanese Immigrant Relations in Rural California, 1900–1913." *Pacific Historical Review*78, no. 2 (May 2009).

United States Immigration Commission, Immigrants in Industries, Part 23–25: Japanese and Other Immigrant races in the Pacific Coast and Rocky Mountain States. Washington DC, 1911.

United States War Liquidation Agency. "People in Motion: The Postwar Adjustment of Evacuated Japanese Americans." United States Department of the Interior, 1947.

Uno, Kathleen. "The Death of "Good Wife, Wise Mother"?" In *Postwar Japan as History*, ed. Andrew Gordon. Berkeley: University of California Press, 1993.

Van Sant, John. *Pacific Pioneers: Japanese Journeys to America and Hawaii, 1850–1880*. Urbana: University of Illinois Press, 2000.

Wagatsuma, Hiroshi. "The Social Perception of Skin Color," *Daedalus* 96, no. 2 (Spring 1967): 418.

Wallenstein, Peter. *Tell the Court I Love My Wife: Race, Marriage, and Law—An American History*. New York: Palgrave Macmillan, 2002.

Washington Post. "War Bride Tries to Kill Children, Self." May 19, 1957.

Waswo, Ann and Nishida Yoshiaki. *Farmers and Village Life in Japan*. London: Routledge, 2003.

Wentworth Smith, Janet and William L. Worden, "They're Bringing Home Japanese Wives." *Saturday Evening Post*, January 19, 1952.

Williams, Teresa. "Marriage Between Japanese Women and U.S. Servicemen Since WWII," *Amerasia Journal* 17, no. 1 (1991).

Wilson, L. Alex. "24th Infantry GI's Lovesick . . . 400 to Wed Tokyo Girls." *The Chicago Defender*, November 4, 1950.

Wiltse, Jeff. *Contested Waters: A Social History of Swimming Pools in America*. Chapel Hill: University of North Carolina Press, 2007.

Wolgin, Philip E. and Irene Bloemraad. "'Our Gratitude to Our Soldiers': Military Spouses, Family Re-Unification, and Postwar Immigration Reform." *Journal of Interdisciplinary History* 4, no. 1 (2010).

Yamamoto, Hisaye. "Las Vegas Charley." In *Seventeen Syllables and Other Stories*, ed. Robert Rolf and Hisaye Yamamoto. New Brunswick, NJ: Rutgers University Press, 2010.

Yeager, Chris. "Jero: Japan's First African-American Enka Singer." *Japan America Society of Greater Philadelphia, Konnichiwa Philadelphia*, July 2, 2008.

Yoshida, Reiji. "Letters from Kobe, Young reckless, Open-eyed GIs broke social taboos, found war brides, racist laws, VD." *Japan Times*, September 9, 2008.

Yuh, Ji-Yeon. *Beyond the Shadow of Camptown: Korean Military Brides in America*. New York: New York University Press, 2004.

Zeiger, Sandra. *Entangling Alliances: Foreign War Brides and American Soldiers in the Twentieth Century*. New York: New York University Press, 2010.

INDEX

Page numbers in *italics* indicate figures.

ABOUT THE AUTHOR

SONIA C. GOMEZ is Assistant Professor of US History at Santa Clara University where she teaches courses on migration, intimacy, and social movements. She earned a PhD from the University of Chicago and a BA from the University of California, Berkeley. Her maternal grandmother, Michiko Ikeda, was a Japanese war bride and the source of inspiration for this book.